What people are saying about

7 SECRETS of CONFESSION

(Excerpts from some of the reviews received.
Full reviews can be found at www.mercysong.com)

"Those who read this short but insightful book should be able to approach the sacrament of Confession with greater love, fervor and gratitude. I am happy to recommend it to every Catholic and confessor."

~**Cardinal Donald Wuerl,** Archbishop of Washington

"Vinny Flynn is my favorite Catholic writer, bar none. In *7 Secrets of Confession*, he addresses the most misunderstood sacrament of the Church, and his readers will never look at confession the same way again.

~**Felix Carroll,** Author, *Lost, Loved, Found:
17 Divine Mercy Conversions*

"Truly wonderful! Vinny Flynn has given us a gift — for every soul, for every fallen-away child, parent, friend and enemy, and for every faithful Catholic."

~**Mother Miriam of the Lamb of God, O.S.B.**
Daughters of Mary, Mother of Israel's Hope
www.motherofisraelshope.org

"I will approach Confession in a whole new light of truth because of this book!"

~**Kathleen Beckman,** Radio Maria Host, *Living Eucharist*,
Author, *Rekindle Eucharistic Amazement*

"I encourage everybody, Catholics and non-Catholics alike, to read and reflect on these *7 Secrets* — especially all pastors of souls, formators, and teachers of the faith. This book should be found in every Formation House, Seminary, Religious Community and Parish House."

~The Most Reverend (Dr.) Martin Igwe Uzoukwu
Catholic Bishop of Minna, Nigeria,
Founder, Missionaries of Divine Mercy

"Brace yourself, and don't say you haven't been warned. In *7 Secrets of Confession*, Vinny Flynn will guide you to a closer relationship with Jesus and a deeper appreciation for this important sacrament. This book will definitely be on my 'best of 2013' list."

~Sarah Reinhard, Blogger at SnoringScholar.com
Author of *A Catholic Mother's Companion to Pregnancy*

"A phenomenal book! It will touch the hearts and minds of the Faithful of all ages, helping them to understand, in simple but profound terms, the beauty of the Sacrament of Healing and Mercy."

~Fr. Gary M. Dailey, Director of Vocations
Diocese of Springfield, Mass.

"As someone who's had a love-hate-love relationship with confession for many years, I can vouch for the power of Vinny Flynn's amazing *7 Secrets of Confession* to change hearts and minds."

~Lisa M. Hendey, Founder of CatholicMom.com
Author of *A Book of Saints for Catholic Moms*

"No matter which side of the confessional grille you're on, Vinny Flynn's *7 Secrets of Confession* is an indispensable guide to the sacrament of Reconciliation."

"You are going to love Vinny Flynn's latest gem, *7 Secrets of Confession!* In an age in which the sacrament of Reconciliation is so often misunderstood, neglected, and even ignored, this book offers invaluable insights."

"With clarity, charity, and insight, Vinny Flynn has written a beautiful book designed to bring Catholics more deeply into one of the great gifts of the Heart of Jesus — the sacrament of Confession."

"Confession is one of the most powerful of all the sacraments, yet is sadly neglected in our world today. In *7 Secrets of Confession*, Vinny Flynn provides a down-to-earth presentation that unveils its deep beauty and leads us to a more accurate mindset. Seeing confession through the eyes of God's mercy, we come to desire it the way we desire Communion."

7 Secrets of Confession

Vinny Flynn

Introduction by Fr. Michael Gaitley, MIC

MercySong
STOCKBRIDGE, MASSACHUSETTS

PUBLISHED BY MERCYSONG, INC.
Stockbridge, Massachusetts USA
www.mercysong.com

IN COLLABORATION WITH IGNATIUS PRESS
San Francisco, California, USA

Published with Ecclesiastical approval
Nihil Obstat
Reverend Mark S. Stelzer, S.T.D.
Censor Librorum
Diocese of Springfield in Massachusetts
Nativity of St. John the Baptist
June 24, 2013

Library of Congress Catalog Card No: 2013911654

ISBN: 978-1-884479-46-5

7 Secrets logo: Riz Boncan Marsella
Design by Mary Flannery

Cover art from "The Love That Saves," © 2013 by Maria Rangel
www.rangelstudios.com.

PRINTED IN THE UNITED STATES OF AMERICA
August, 2013

To Fr. Peter, OFM

*my confessor and lifelong friend, who has
laughed and cried and prayed with me,
reflected to me the merciful face of the Father,
and walked patiently with me on the
path to healing and holiness.*

Special Thanks

To my beloved daughter and dedicated editor,
Erin Flynn, who kept me on track
and worked so closely and indispensably
with me throughout the entire writing,
editing, and production process.

To David Came, executive editor of Marian Press,
who, in spite of his own busy schedule,
made the time to review the manuscript
and provide us with invaluable editorial
assistance in preparing it for publication.

"While we can still be healed,
let us surrender ourselves
into the hands of our
Divine Physician."

— From a 2nd century homily

CONTENTS

Author's Note

Quotations used in the text are generally arranged by page number and section in the Notes, Sources, and References at the end. Quotations from Scripture, the *Catechism of the Catholic Church*, some Church documents, and the *Diary of St. Faustina* are cited in the text itself.

$\mathcal{I}$NTRODUCTION

"Fear is useless. What is needed is trust."

Mark 5:36

In the *Diary of St. Faustina*, Jesus tells us, **"Pray for souls that they be not afraid to approach the tribunal of My mercy"** (975). I believe that people *have* been praying for this intention and that this book will help many come back to confession.

When I was in the seminary, I used to go to confession every Saturday morning, even though I didn't have to. It was my weekly meeting with Jesus to encounter His love in the Sacrament of Mercy, and it gave me so much peace and joy. But getting there wasn't easy. Nearly every time, before confessing, there'd be a barrage of what I believe were spiritual attacks.

The most common attack was fear, and it usually hit me as I was waiting in the confession line. In fact, the closer I got to the confessional, the more the fear would grow, usually accompanied by thoughts such as, "The priest is going to yell at you." … "You're the worst sinner; there's no mercy for you." … "You won't remember any of your sins and will look like such a fool. "… "He's going to be shocked at your sins." … "You just confess the same sins over and over, and this time God has had enough of you."

These thoughts and the waves of anxiety that accompanied them did not make sense. After all, for years I'd had a great devotion to the message of Divine Mercy. My image of God was most definitely the image of Jesus full of love and mercy.

Yet, despite everything I knew of His mercy, I couldn't always shake these thoughts and fears. I'd fight them by praying what had become my constant prayer, "Jesus, I trust in You" — but it wasn't easy. It was like every time I got into the confession line, amnesia would set in, and I'd forget all I'd learned about God's mercy.

Then, one day, I read a passage from the *Diary of St. Faustina* that has helped me perhaps more than any other. Jesus said to Faustina:

> Every time you go to confession, immerse yourself entirely in My mercy, with great trust, so that I may pour the bounty of My grace upon your soul. ... Tell souls that from this fount of mercy souls draw graces solely with the vessel of trust. If their trust is great, there is no limit to My generosity.
>
> 1602

No wonder the weekly attacks focused on fear! Satan wanted to rob me of the graces of confession, and he knew that fear kills trust. So, after reading this passage, I made a firm resolution to approach the confessional in the same way I approach Jesus — with contrition and great trust in his mercy. That resolution has helped, but there's often still a battle.

Thanks to *7 Secrets of Confession*, the battle has become easier to fight. Vinny's "7 Secrets" are like seven explosions that blow away the obstacles keeping us from the Sacrament of Mercy. If you've ever dragged your feet on the way to confession, gotten discouraged about confessing the same sins over and over, or wondered how your confessions could be more fruitful, then you'll love this book. It turns what many see as a tiresome obligation into a precious, longed-for encounter with the Lord.

Whether you go to confession every week or haven't been in many years, this book will help you rediscover and fall deeply in love with the gift of God's mercy in this incredible sacrament. I'm deeply grateful that Vinny hasn't kept these secrets to himself. And when you read this book, you'll be grateful, too. It truly is an answer to prayer.

Fr. Michael Gaitley, MIC

Father Michael Gaitley is the director of The Association of Marian Helpers in Stockbridge, Mass. An extremely gifted writer and popular speaker, he has authored several books, including *33 Days to Morning Glory*, *Consoling the Heart of Jesus*, and *The 'One Thing' Is Three*. He has also created a comprehensive, parish-based program for the New Evangelization, called Hearts Afire (www.AllHeartsAfire.com).

FOREWORD
Beyond the Grocery List

> **With joy and trust
> let us rediscover
> this sacrament.**
>
> Pope John Paul II

L et's start by being honest. Confession was never my idea of a fun thing to do on a Saturday afternoon. Or any other time, for that matter.

Somehow, the prospect of telling another human being things I didn't even want to admit to myself wasn't very exciting. It was always awkward, often difficult, and sometimes downright humiliating — especially when the priest was less than patient and understanding.

I "Have to Go"

But, being a "good Catholic," I wanted to receive Communion, and I knew I couldn't rightfully do that if I had serious sin on my soul. So, whenever I became conscious that I had committed serious sin, my guilt would prod me to go to confession.

This is what confession meant to me. I never thought of it as something to be desired just for itself. It was simply a means to an end, a way to have my sins forgiven so I could worthily receive Communion. Sure, sometimes I'd feel better afterwards, but I still wouldn't have gone if I didn't feel I had to.

There were even times when my regret for my sins was caused more by the thought of my having to go to confession than by any feeling of right or wrong, or of what I would now call true contrition. Instead of "Oh, no! I've offended God," it was "Oh, no! Now I have to go to confession."

Confession and Communion were two entirely different things to me, and their only relationship was that one was the prerequisite for the other. I *wanted* to receive Communion, so I *had* to go to confession.

"Grocery List" Confession

Because of the limited understanding I had about confession, my whole focus was on sin, which to me simply meant bad behavior. It was when I was *bad* in "thought, word, or deed."

So I kept a list in my mind, a "grocery list" of bad thoughts, words, and actions. When there were too many items on my list, or when one of the items seemed *too* bad, I'd realize that I shouldn't go to Communion until I had been to confession. So I'd gather up my courage and force myself to enter the confessional, hoping the priest wouldn't know who I was. Sound familiar?

In my mind, God was only indirectly involved. Confession was between me and the priest. I'd rattle off my grocery list of sins and recite the little Act of Contrition prayer I had memorized as a child. The priest would then forgive me in the name of God and give me a penance to do; and I'd leave the confessional with a sense of relief, knowing I was starting over and could receive Communion once again.

Was this all bad? Of course not. We need to have an awareness of sin and forgiveness. And it certainly would have been wrong for me to receive Communion if I had serious sin on my soul.

But my understanding of confession was so limited and narrow in its focus that it kept me from discovering the real beauty and value of this sacrament — beauty and value that even a young child can learn to understand if it's presented properly.

During the last few years, as I've traveled around the country giving talks and missions, I've come to realize that many Catholics have this same limited understanding of confession, and that there's a great need for clear teaching about this great sacrament.

Rediscovering the "Secrets"

As I explained in my earlier book *7 Secrets of the Eucharist*, there are no real secrets here, but simply truths that for some reason have lain hidden in the heart of the Church and need to be rediscovered.

"Now more than ever," writes Pope John Paul II, "the People of God must be helped to rediscover … the sacrament of mercy." And he adds,

> Let us ask Christ to help us to rediscover the full beauty of this sacrament … to abandon ourselves to the mercy of God … and with his grace set out again on our journey to holiness.

So, if you have not yet experienced confession as a wonderful, personal encounter with God; if you do not yet look forward to going to confession with the same eagerness and expectation with which you go to receive Communion, then please read on. It may change your life.

SECRET 1

Sin Doesn't Change God

God is not subject to eclipse or change.
He is forever one and the same. … I trust in You,
Jesus, for You are unchangeable. …
You are always the same, full of mercy.

St. Faustina, Diary 386, 1489

To really understand confession, we need to understand sin. We need to realize what sin *is*, what it *does*, and (perhaps most importantly) what it *doesn't do*.

As I mentioned in the Foreword, I used to think of sin simply as bad behavior. It was when I thought or said or did something wrong. Gradually, I learned to think of these bad behaviors as also offenses against God. Little offenses were "venial sins," and they only bothered God a little. Serious offenses were "mortal sins," and, in addition to preventing me from receiving Communion, they made God really mad at me. Confession, along with the penance that the priest would give me, was something I had to do to "make up for" what I had done, so that I could go to Communion and so that God wouldn't be mad at me anymore.

How wrong I was! Sin isn't just about behavior; it's about relationship.

You and I are not here by accident. And we weren't created absent-mindedly by a God who was just playing with clay because He was bored and had nothing else to do.

We exist because God is a Father who wanted children — children whom He created "in his own image and likeness" (Gen 1:26-27) so that they could receive His love and ultimately come to share in His own divine life in the Trinity.

As Pope John Paul II writes in his encyclical

letter, *Rich in Mercy,* God is not merely the creator:

> He is also Father: He is linked to man
> … by a bond still more intimate than that of
> creation. It is love, which not only creates
> the good but also grants participation in the
> very life of God. … For he who loves desires
> to give himself.

#7

And Pope Benedict XVI, in his first homily as pope, adds,

> We are not some casual and meaningless
> product of evolution. Each of us is the result
> of a thought of God. Each of us is willed,
> each of us is loved.

Wow! You exist because God thought of you and loved you! This God, this Father, who willed us into life and longs to give Himself to us, has revealed, over and over again, that His love for each of us is personal and forever, and that His focus is not on our behavior but on our relationship with Him.

God has not simply created us, but has fathered us, and He continues to father us forever:

"I have loved you with an everlasting love" (Jer 31:3 RSV).

"See, upon the palms of my hands, I have written your name" (Is 49:16).

"Though the mountains leave their place and the hills be shaken, my love shall never leave you" (Is 54:10).

"I will be a father to you, and you shall be sons and daughters to me" (2 Cor 6:18).

How does this relate to sin? Sin is when we refuse to let God father us. It's when we fail to respond to His love and guidance, refusing to live in this personal, loving relationship with Him as His sons and daughters. As theologian Scott Hahn expresses it,

> The essence of sin is our refusal of divine sonship.

This refusal, of course, inevitably results in various behaviors which we call sins, but the specific behaviors are not really the problem. They are symptoms or expressions of the problem. The real problem is in our hearts, in our refusal to accept and respond to the Father's love.

Does this refusal, along with the resulting sinful behaviors, change the Father's love and destroy our relationship with Him?

No. And that's the whole point. As Pope John Paul II explains in his reflections on the parable of the prodigal son,

> The father of the prodigal son is faithful to his fatherhood, faithful to the love that he had always lavished on his son.
>
> *Rich in Mercy,* 6

> After all, it was his own son who was involved, and such a relationship could never be altered or destroyed by any sort of behavior.
>
> *Rich in Mercy,* 5

Our behavior, no matter how bad it may be, can never undo the reality of our relationship to God as His children, and *nothing* can ever change His love for us.

As St. Faustina writes,

> Everything may change, but love, never,
> never; it is always the same.
>
> *Diary,* 947

So, if our sinful behavior doesn't change God, doesn't cause Him to withdraw from His relationship with us as a loving Father, then what does it do?

It separates us from His love.

Let's take another look at what sin means. When I was a young man, I heard a priest give a definition of sin that I had never heard before and that was very different from the theologically-oriented definitions I had learned in CCD class:

> Sin is turning your face away from God.

I never forgot that definition. It fits every sin I can imagine. The distinction between venial and mortal sin now became clearer to me as I thought about how many degrees of turning there can be between "facing towards God" and "facing away from God."

The severity of my sin depends on how clearly I realize that I am turning away from God, how consciously and freely I choose to turn away, and how complete the turn is.

The *Catechism of the Catholic Church* presents an additional image that makes the comparison even clearer:

> Sin sets itself against God's love for us and turns our hearts away from it.
>
> #1850

Our *hearts!* Not just our faces. Remember what we saw earlier — that our sinful behaviors are just symptoms of the real problem? The real problem is in our hearts.

When we sin, we turn not only our faces away from God, but the rest of us as well — our minds, our hearts, our spirits.

When we sin, we set ourselves against God's love, and thus we separate ourselves from Him. But the *Catechism* doesn't say that sin sets God against us. It doesn't say that sin turns His heart away from us.

God never causes the separation that results from our sin. He never turns His face or His Heart from us. But, because He has created us free and respects our freedom, he allows us to turn away. Just pause and let that sink in for a minute. *He* doesn't turn away; He allows *us* to turn away.

So what's the remedy? Turn back. Change our hearts and turn back.

A few years ago, at a men's retreat that we were presenting, my son John explained that "conversion" and "repentance" can best be understood by thinking of a military command: "About, FACE!"

He asked for a volunteer, and one of the men who had been in the military came up and demonstrated the proper response to the command.

He did it quite well. It was a crisp, strong, and complete turning of his whole body so that he was facing in the opposite direction.

Since then, whenever I hear the word "convert" or "repent," I think of it as an order (and a loving invitation) from the "Commander-in-Chief" to do an "about-face" and turn back to Him.

We need to understand, more than anything else, that God's love for each of us is permanent. It's forever, and nothing can change that. No sin is greater than His love.

Nothing that you or I have ever done, ever will do,

or ever could do, can make Him stop loving us. We don't have the power to change God! He is always loving us, always the unchangeable "I am" (Ex 3:14).

Remember the scene on the mountain when Moses asked God who He was? God's response always seemed so awkward and confusing to me, and none of the translations made it any clearer:

> I am who I am …
> I am that I am …
> I am who am …
> I am he who is.

All I could get out of it was that God seemed to be emphasizing His own existence — emphasizing perhaps that He is the One who has always existed and will always exist.

Then I heard a scholarly priest explain that it's not possible to translate this passage accurately into English but, if we could, it would come out as "I am the *is-ing* One."

No, that's not a misprint; he really said *is-ing*. I know that in grammar school you probably learned that in English the forms of the verb "to be" do not express action, but simply a state of being.

The priest's point was that God always exists, always "is," but that, in God, existence is not just a state of *being*; it's an *action!*

What *is* God? St. John tells us that "God is love" (1 Jn 4:9). But in God love is not a noun; it's a verb. Yes, God is love, but that love is not static, not just a "state of being." It is always active, always creative, always pouring out for us.

God is never just *being;* He is always *doing.* Love is what God *is* and what He *does* — always and unchangeably. He is always loving us, not because of who we are or how we behave, but rather because that's His nature; that's who He is. He is the "is-ing One," the "Loving One."

St. John of the Cross offers a simple analogy that clarifies this, comparing God to the sun:

> The sun is up early and shining on your house, ready to shine in if you open the curtains. So God, who never sleeps nor slumbers, … is like the sun, shining over souls.

Science tells us that, in reality, the sun never sets,

never "goes down." It's the earth that moves, turning away from the sun. The sun is still doing its thing; it's still shining, giving warmth and light to whomever is there to receive it. In the same way, God is always loving, giving light and warmth to all who are there to receive.

When we separate ourselves from God and His love by sin, it is not God who changes. The change takes place in us.

Most of us haven't really learned that. We've learned that what we do (or don't do) affects the way others respond to us, and that love is something we have to earn with good behavior.

We learn early that parents, teachers, friends, even strangers react positively or negatively to us based on how we act. Even Santa Claus is checking up on us to see whether we've been "naughty or nice." If you're good, you get good things; if you're bad, all you get is coal in your stocking.

Even though we read in Genesis that God created us in His image and likeness (see 1:27), we get it mixed up and think it's OK for us to recreate *Him* in *our* image and likeness. Since we tend to love conditionally, based on behavior, we think He does, too.

So, every once in a while, we look at our behavior and think we're unworthy of His love. Well, guess what? Of course you're unworthy of His love! He's God, and you're just a creature He created out of dust. What could you ever do to become worthy of His love?

The good news is that you don't have to be worthy of His love. He loves you because of who He is and who He created you to be — not just a creature, but His own child. You can't earn God's love, and you can't lose it; you already have it, forever.

But you do have a choice: you can accept it or refuse it. Sin is when you refuse it.

The sun is always shining, always giving heat and light. I can't change that. But I can turn my face away. I can keep the curtains closed. I can put up an umbrella to shade myself from it.

I can even go into a cave and say, "Where did the sun go? Why is it so dark and cold in here?" But the sun hasn't changed. It's still shining, still giving heat and light. And anytime I choose to come out of the cave, it will still be there waiting for me.

But, as long as I stay in the cave, I can't see the sun. I can't experience its warmth and light because I have turned away. In the same way, when I turn away from God by sin, it doesn't change Him. It changes my ability to see, my capacity to experience and receive the love He is endlessly pouring out for me.

St. Theophilus of Antioch writes:

> God is seen by those who have the capacity to see him, provided that they keep the eyes of their mind open. All have eyes, but some have eyes that are shrouded in darkness, unable to see the light of the sun.
>
> Because the blind cannot see it, it does not follow that the sun does not shine. The blind must trace the cause back to themselves and their eyes.
>
> In the same way, you have eyes in your mind that are shrouded in darkness because of your sins and evil deeds. … No one who has sin in him can see God.

Sin is not just "breaking the rules," not just an offense against God. It's also an offense against myself. And it carries with it its own punishment. It imprisons me in the cold darkness of the cave, depriving me of the warmth and light for which I was created.

> Sin brings me into the cave.
> Confession brings me out.

SIN DOESN'T CHANGE GOD

$\mathcal{S}$ECRET 2
It's Not Just about Forgiveness

*We come to confession
to be healed.*

St. Faustina, Diary, 377

At countless talks, retreats, and missions I've asked thousands of people a simple question: "If you could only use one word to explain the purpose of confession, what would that word be?

The answer is always the same: *forgiveness*.

But it's the wrong answer.

Now don't burn me at the stake yet. Of course

confession is about forgiveness. But that's just one part of a much broader purpose, and the word that best expresses that purpose is *healing*.

For much of my life, as I mentioned in the Foreword, whenever I thought about confession, my whole focus was on sin, which to me meant bad behavior.

I didn't go to confession on any regular basis. I went only when I realized I had serious sins to confess, and my main purpose for going was to get my sins forgiven so I could receive Communion.

I don't mean to imply that it was simply a cold, mechanical process for me. I thought I was being a good Catholic. At some level, I understood that my sins were offenses against God and, when I would recite the Act of Contrition, I meant it. I was sorry for my sins, and I wanted to try to do better.

So, I'd go into the confessional with my little (or sometimes big) grocery list of sins, recite them to the priest, say the Act of Contrition, and receive absolution.

Were my sins forgiven? Of course. But the next time I'd go back to confession, guess what? Same list.

Whenever I ask that question during a talk, many people usually give the answer before I do, and there are always a lot of knowing smiles and nodding heads. So I feign surprise and ask, "How did you know?" Obviously, I'm not the only one who has experienced the "same list" syndrome. It seems to be a common problem.

Why do we tend to keep coming back with the same list?

There are probably a lot of reasons, including the reality of human weakness and the "inclination to sin" that the Church calls "concupiscence," which remains with us even after baptism as we struggle to reach the holiness to which the Lord calls us (see *Catechism*, #1426).

And as one priest told me, we shouldn't get too depressed about our tendency to give in to the same weaknesses. "After all," he asked with a smile, "you wouldn't want to keep coming back with *new* sins, would you?"

But I think the main reason we keep returning with the same list is that we don't understand what Christ wants to do in the confessional. We go simply wanting our sins forgiven, not realizing that He wants to do much more. He wants to heal us of the attitudes, disordered desires, problems, and wounds that are causing us to keep committing those sins.

And, just in case you're wondering, this isn't just my personal "Psych 101" view of confession. It's the clear teaching of the Church. If you look for information about confession in the *Catechism*, you won't find it under "Forgiveness." You'll find it under "Sacraments of Healing."

Let's take a quick look at the purpose of the sacraments. Every sacrament, as the old *Baltimore Catechism* so clearly explained, is "an outward sign instituted by Christ to give grace."

"To give grace." What's grace? We Christians tend to use this word a lot, but I've rarely found anyone who can really explain what grace is.

I always viewed grace in a pretty vague way as a kind of help that God gives us. And there's certainly some truth in this. Indeed, it's the first definition given in the *Catechism*, which calls it "the free and undeserved help that God gives us" (#1996).

But the *Catechism* goes on to explain *why* God

gives it to us. It's so that we can "become children of God," sharing in His divine nature and starting to live eternal life *now* (#1996).

> Grace is a participation in the life of God. It introduces us into the intimacy of Trinitarian life.
>
> #1997

So grace isn't just help; it's actually a new kind of life — God's eternal life, poured into our soul "to heal it of sin and to sanctify it" (#1999) so that we can become like Him and live the way He lives.

To heal it of sin and to sanctify it! Notice that the *Catechism* doesn't say to *forgive* it of sin, but to *heal and sanctify* (make holy).

What does all this mean? It means that, since the purpose of every sacrament is to give grace, and the purpose of grace is to heal and sanctify, then the ultimate goal of each sacrament is to heal us and make us holy so that we can become like God.

But each of the sacraments also has its own specific character, effects, and forms of celebration.

Baptism, Confirmation, and Eucharist, for example, are called sacraments of Christian initiation, because their particular focus is to get us started in a Christian way of living and to give us all the graces we need to persevere and grow in that way of life (see *Catechism*, #1212, 1533).

Holy Orders and Matrimony are focused on helping others receive salvation and, to that end, these sacraments confer a very particular consecration upon those who receive them, enabling them to fulfil the specific duties of their state of life (see *Catechism*, #1534-35).

The other two sacraments are called sacraments of healing, because they are specifically directed toward continuing Christ's ministry of healing.

So although the ultimate goal of each sacrament is healing and holiness, the sacrament of Reconciliation is one of the two sacraments *specifically* directed toward that goal:

> The Lord Jesus Christ, physician of our souls and bodies, who forgave the sins of the paralytic and restored him to bodily health, has willed that his Church continue, in the power of the Holy Spirit, his work of

> healing and salvation. ... This is the pur-
> pose of the two sacraments of healing: the
> sacrament of Penance and the sacrament of
> Anointing of the Sick.
>
> *Catechism*, #1421

I love this passage from the *Catechism*, because it presents the image of Christ, not as a harsh judge, but as the great physician who has the authority and power to heal both our souls and our bodies.

The passage references the wonderful gospel scene of the paralyzed man whose friends are trying to bring him to Jesus, but can't get to Him because of the crowds. Not to be deterred, they make an opening in the roof of the building in which Jesus is preaching, and lower him down to Jesus.

They are hoping, of course, that Jesus will heal him of his physical paralysis, but Jesus surprises everyone by first forgiving his sins and only then healing his body (see Mk 2:3-5).

There's so much to learn from this scene. The two actions are not unrelated. They are both performed by Jesus in his capacity as "physician of our souls and bodies," emphasizing that physical sickness is often somehow related to spiritual sickness, and that sin, in a very real sense, can paralyze us.

Christ's forgiveness of the man's sins can be seen as a necessary first step toward the complete healing that is realized when his physical paralysis is also cured. As the *Catechism* points out,

> God's forgiveness initiates the healing. … He has come to heal the whole man, soul and body; he is the physician the sick have need of.
>
> #1502, 1503

Okay, before we go any further, we need to clear up two common misconceptions. The first concerns the relationship between physical ailments and sin. There is a very real connection between soul and body, and as I mentioned above, "physical sickness is often somehow related to spiritual sickness." But this does not mean that every time you're sick it's because of some sin you've committed. Christ makes this very clear after another dramatic healing, the healing of the man born blind.

As they passed by the man, Christ's disciples, influenced by the rigid teaching of the rabbis, which held that every sickness is caused by someone's sin, ask Jesus whose sin is to blame.

Jesus rejects the erroneous teaching and makes it clear that sickness is not necessarily caused by sin, but can be allowed — and in some cases, healed — as a part of God's plan and purpose:

> His disciples asked him, "Rabbi, who sinned, this man or his parents, that he was born blind?" Jesus answered, "Neither he nor his parents sinned; it is so that the works of God might be made visible through him."
>
> John 9: 2-3

Jesus then heals the man by restoring his sight, but only after announcing Himself as "the light of the world" (Jn 9:5). The healing of the man's physical blindness thus proves Christ's claim to be the light of the world and symbolically reveals His ability and intent to provide enlightenment and healing for our spiritual blindness as well.

The second misconception involves an important distinction between a healing and a cure. Because the scriptures provide us with so many examples of dramatic physical healings, we can be led to believe that all healing involves a physical cure. But this is not true. Christ's touch *always* brings healing, especially through the sacraments, in which He "continues to 'touch' us in order to heal us" (*Catechism* #1504). At times, as in the examples we've just seen, His healing also includes a physical cure. But His main concern is always to heal our spiritual sickness, the moral misery that comes from sin.

Christ does not always cure specific ailments. He always offers His healing love to those who suffer, but He does not always alleviate their suffering or cure their infirmities.

> Moved by so much suffering, Christ not only allows himself to be touched by the sick, but he makes their miseries his own: "He took our infirmities and bore our diseases." But he did not heal all the sick. His healings were signs of the coming of the Kingdom of God. They announced a more radical healing: the victory over sin and death.
>
> *Catechism* #1505

Christ, Himself, emphasizing the relationship between sin and moral sickness, explicitly identified His ministry as one of spiritual healing. When the Pharisees criticized Him for associating with known sinners, he responded:

> Those who are well have no need of a physician, but those who are sick. ... I have come not to call the righteous, but sinners.
>
> Matthew 9: 12-13 NRSV

This image of Christ as physician reoccurs throughout the *Catechism* and is specifically related to Christ's healing ministry through the sacrament of Reconcilation. In the confessional,

> He is the physician tending each one of the sick who need him to cure them.
>
> #1484

St. Faustina, in her teaching about confession, also emphasizes the healing nature of this sacrament and provides additional insights into its purpose and effects.

She explains that we should come to confession for two purposes:

> 1. We come to confession to be healed;
> 2. We come to be educated — like a small child, our soul has constant need of education.
>
> *Diary*, 377

Healing and education. Notice that she doesn't even mention sin and forgiveness. Why not?

Because she knows that sin wounds us and that, even after our sins are forgiven, we remain wounded, confused, and spiritually weak.

Forgiveness of our sins is absolutely necessary for our salvation, which is why we need to confess our sins. But we need to understand that forgiveness is not the exclusive or final goal of confession. It's the necessary first step in a whole process. As we have already seen from the *Catechism*, "Forgiveness initiates the healing" (#1502).

We need to rid ourselves of the simplistic view of confession as some kind of magic formula that gives us an instant "fix" for sin:

> Oops, I messed up again and fell into serious sin. … OK, into the confessional,

rattle off my sins to the priest. He recites the words of absolution, waves his hand over me in blessing, and 'poof!' My sins are forgiven. There! I'm all better now.

But I'm not all better! And neither are you. Forgiveness alone is just not enough, because our woundedness and lack of understanding make it too hard for us to avoid further sin.

Confession is not meant to be a quick fix! It's meant to be a *process* of healing and education that helps us grow so that we don't keep falling again and again into the same old habits of sin — same list.

I'll bet when you were first learning how to go to confession, nobody told you that part of the process was about education. But Pope John Paul II refers to confession as "a sacrament of enlightenment … a precious light for the path of perfection." And Pope Benedict XVI is even more specific, stressing that the priest is not just there to grant absolution, but is "called to take on the role of father, spiritual guide, teacher, and educator."

For me, the lyrics of an old hymn best capture what Christ wants to do for us through confession:

> Praise my soul the King of Heaven;
> To His feet your tribute bring;
> Ransomed, healed, restored, forgiven,
> Evermore His praises sing

"Ransomed, healed, restored, forgiven." This is what is supposed to happen for you and me in the confessional.

Ransomed? Yes! You've been kidnapped. Your sins are holding you captive in the kingdom of darkness. On the cross, Christ paid your ransom of justice to the Father. By taking upon Himself the just punishment your sins deserved, and offering His suffering to the Father in atonement for your sins, He won forgiveness for you and rescued you.

But you are still wounded and weak, and you have lost much — your health, your strength, your innocence, your likeness to God — so you need to be not only forgiven, but healed and restored.

The *Catechism* gives a clear explanation of the effects of sin and of the desire of Jesus to restore us:

> Disfigured by sin and death, man remains "in the image of God," in the image

of the Son, but is deprived "of the glory of God," of his "likeness." ...

The Son himself will assume that "image" and restore it in the Father's "likeness'" by giving it again its Glory, the Spirit who is "the giver of life."

#705

When we sin, we wound ourselves; we disfigure ourselves, so that, though we were created to be like God, we don't resemble Him anymore. We don't *look* like Him, we don't *think* like Him, we don't *act* like Him.

Jesus wants to restore us in the Father's likeness. How? Through the sacrament of Reconciliation. He told St. Faustina that the greatest miracles take place in the confessional, and that there is no sinner who cannot be restored:

> Were a soul like a decaying corpse so that from a human standpoint there would be no [hope of] restoration and everything would already be lost, it is not so with God. The miracle of Divine Mercy restores that soul in full.
>
> *Diary* , 1448

As I mentioned in Secret 1, God's focus is not on our sin, but on our relationship with Him. He's focused on our pain — on our woundedness. He knows what sin is! He knows that sin is misery, that it's sickness. He knows that we're aching, and He wants to heal us, to restore all that has been lost.

Let's take another look at the parable of the prodigal son. Having turned away from his father, the son ends up squandering his inheritance and losing everything, and he is ultimately reduced to complete poverty and hunger.

But hidden beneath the surface of these material losses, lies a greater tragedy, "the tragedy of lost dignity, the awareness of squandered sonship" (*Rich in Mercy*, # 5).

At first it seems that the son's decision to return to his father is prompted only by hunger and poverty, but Pope John Paul II points out that this motive "is permeated by an awareness of a deeper loss," the loss of his dignity as a son.

The son realizes that because of his sin, his willful rejection of his father, he no longer deserves to be his father's son:

> Father, I have sinned against heaven and
> against you. I no longer deserve to be called
> your son.
>
> Luke 15:21

But what he doesn't realize until his father runs to embrace him is that mercy goes beyond justice; it is love poured out upon those who don't deserve it.

> Love is transformed into mercy when it
> is necessary to go beyond the precise norms
> of justice — precise and often too narrow.
>
> *Rich in Mercy*, #5

> This love is able to reach down to every
> prodigal son, to every human misery, and
> above all to every form of moral misery, to
> sin. When this happens, the person who is
> the object of mercy does not feel humiliated,
> but rather found again and "restored to
> value."
>
> *Rich in Mercy*, #6

So, if this is really what God wants, if He's not focused on our sin, but simply wants to heal us and restore us (even though we don't deserve it), then why do we have to confess our sins?

Because God created us free, and He won't force anything on us, not even His love, His forgiveness, His healing. When we're sick, we need to go to the doctor:

> When Christ's faithful strive to confess all the sins that they can remember, they undoubtedly place all of them before The Divine Mercy for pardon.
>
> But those who fail to do so and knowingly withhold some, place nothing before the Divine Goodness for remission through the mediation of the priest. For if the sick person is too ashamed to show his wound to the doctor, the medicine cannot heal what it does not know.
>
> *Catechism*, #1456

Perhaps the best example of this is the story of the Pharisee and the tax collector (see Lk 18:9-14). The tax collector, in his humility of heart, knows he's a sinner. He knows he's sick, so he asks the Lord for mercy. The Pharisee, full of pride, thinks he's healthy:

> *"Hi doc. I feel great. I'm sure glad I'm not sick like that poor tax collector."*

Blinded by his arrogance and pride, the Pharisee doesn't recognize the sad state of his own soul. He can't receive healing because he doesn't know he's sick and doesn't express any need.

Pope Benedict XVI, in one of his *Angelus* addresses, gives a powerful teaching about how this type of moral blindness can block the healing that Christ wants to give us through confession.

Referring to the gospel story we saw earlier where Christ heals the man born blind, the pope explains:

> To the blind man whom he healed, Jesus reveals that he has come into the world for judgment, to separate the blind who can be healed from those who do not allow themselves to be healed because they presume they are healthy. … Let us allow Jesus to heal us, Jesus who can and wants to give us the light of God! Let us confess our blindness.

As the *Catechism* simply expresses it:

> In confession, we let ourselves be healed by Christ.
>
> #1458

If we go into the confessional simply to confess our sins and receive forgiveness, we limit the experience that God wants for us.

But if we go in confessing everything — yes, our sins, but also our misery: our sickness, our brokenness, our woundedness — then we not only receive forgiveness but also initiate a process of deep healing that will restore us as children of the Father.

No image of confession is as powerful for me as the image of the prodigal son wrapped in the arms of his father. Confession is when our misery meets His mercy, and all is restored in the Father's embrace.

IT'S NOT JUST ABOUT FORGIVENESS

$\mathcal{S}$ECRET 3

Your Sin is Different from My Sin

*Much will be required of the person
entrusted with much, and still more will be
demanded of the person entrusted with more.*

Luke 12:48

Making an examen of conscience before going to confession used to be fairly easy for me. Thanks to a moral upbringing and the good example of my parents, my conscience had been well-formed, and I had a strong sense of right and wrong. From CCD classes in grammar school and theology classes in high school, I knew the Ten Commandments and had learned the basic teachings of the Church. Since, at that time, I only thought of sin as bad behavior, it was a fairly simple process to identify the things I had done wrong and to classify them in my mind as mortal or venial.

But once I began to realize that sin is not just bad behavior but a refusal of God's love, and that confession is not just about forgiveness but about healing, everything changed. My examen now became more complicated — and much more fruitful.

My list still included behaviors, but now I also had to consider anything that seemed wrong in my relationship with God. I had to look deeper into my daily life and ask myself some hard questions:

In what areas of my life am I not at peace? Where am I angry, depressed, discouraged, anxious, bitter, resentful? Where am I too focused on myself? What areas of my life, my thoughts, my desires, have I not yet given over to Jesus as Lord? What wouldn't I want to talk to Jesus about? What would I not want Him to see? In what ways am I not responding to what God wants me to do?

As I began asking these kinds of questions, I gradually learned to recognize what Fr. David Knight calls the "roots" of bad behavior, the roots of sin:

> "... distorted attitudes, false values, wrong priorities, unconquered appetites, or destructive desires."

As I grew in this deeper awareness of sin, I had to let go of the misconception that sin is always the same.

There are certain acts that are wrong, and they are always wrong. If they are classified by the Church as venial sins, they are always venial, and if they are classified as mortal, they are always mortal — no matter who commits them, no matter why they commit them, no matter what the circumstances. Sin is sin, right?

Wrong! The Church's classification of sins is important and can be a great help in forming a right conscience and identifying problem areas in our lives. But the Church's teaching about sin goes far beyond a mere rigid arrangement of behavior into categories.

Yes, of course, there are actions that are intrinsically evil. Truth is not relative; it does not change with time or circumstances. If something is a wrong action, it is always a wrong action. But sin is not the same for everyone. What's sinful for me may not be sinful for you; what's a mortal sin for me may only be a venial sin for you.

If this doesn't make sense to you yet, don't panic, and don't throw me to the lions. Hang in there with me, and let's take a look at Church teaching.

At the beginning of its teaching on sin in Article 8, the *Catechism of the Catholic Church* reminds us of some basic truths: sin is real; we are all guilty of it; its effects are so deadly that Christ had to die to save us from them; and in order to receive the benefits of Christ's saving action, we have to acknowledge our faults and confess them as sins:

> To receive his mercy, we must admit our faults. "If we say we have no sin, we deceive ourselves, and the truth is not in us" (1 Jn1:8).
>
> #1847

One of the things that can keep us from acknowledging our sins is the failure to acknowledge God.

We are living in a global society in which the problem is not that people don't believe in God; it's that even many "religious," practicing Christians are simply ignoring Him in their daily lives. As Pope John Paul II writes:

> To sin is not merely to deny God. To sin is also to live as if he did not exist, to eliminate him from one's daily life.
>
> *Reconciliation and Penance*, #18

He explains that living in such a society results in a "gradual loss of the sense of sin." By depersonalizing our relationship with God, we end up losing the awareness of personal responsibility for our actions.

Sin is real. We all do it. And it happens when we turn our backs on God or live as if His existence has no bearing on our lives. We need to realize that every action either strengthens our relationship with God or weakens it.

It's this intensely personal, one-on-one relationship with God that we need to keep in mind if we want to understand sin. Where there are no persons, there is no sin. Think about that for a minute. It takes a *person* to commit sin! And every sin is a personal rejection of the specific, unique, and intimate relationship with God to which we are each called.

If we focus only on behavior, viewing sin merely as bad actions and making judgments based only on the classification of these actions as mortal or venial, we miss the deeper reality. We can't depersonalize sin. The central focus must always be on our person-to-person relationship with God.

Does this mean that the Church is wrong to identify specific behaviors as mortal or venial and to assign different degrees of seriousness to them, so that we view some actions as "little" sins and others as "serious" sins?

Of course not. The Church rightly presents the classifications of sin as a guide for us, especially in forming our consciences and developing a clear sense of right and wrong. But this is just a starting point. We also need to grow in our understanding of what's behind the rules, why they were given to us, and how they directly relate to who we are and who we are called to be — with God and with each other.

When we get stuck in the rules, without this

deeper understanding, we become too narrow and legalistic, thinking just about behavior and forgetting about God, except as the one who will punish or reward us.

> "Oh, this is just a venial sin," we think. "It's not really important. God won't be too mad. But this other act would be a mortal sin and would deserve serious punishment."

If we allow ourselves to think this way, viewing only the rightness or wrongness of the action itself, without considering the individual person and the particular circumstances, we miss the most important part of Church teaching.

An action doesn't become a mortal or a venial sin because of what it *is* (and therefore what punishment it deserves), but rather because of what it *does*. Venial sins and mortal sins *do* different things.

What a difference this understanding can make! God has poured His love into our hearts, and we are called to live in that love and express it through our actions (charity). The Church teaches that each venial sin wounds or weakens this charity inside me.

But mortal sin doesn't merely wound charity; it *destroys* it (see *Catechism*, #1855).

This is not just some abstract theological teaching; it's very real! Ever notice that when you fall into serious sin, you find yourself being more impatient, unloving, judgmental, apathetic? Of course! The charity in your heart has been destroyed!

So what makes a sin mortal? Three things:

> 1. The action is a *grave (very serious) violation* that is deadly to my soul because it kills the love that God has placed in my heart and separates me from Him;

> 2. I *know* how serious it is, how opposed it is to God's law;

> 3 In spite of this complete awareness, I make a *personal, deliberate choice* to do it anyway.

> See *Catechism*, #1857

What makes this "grave violation" of God's law mortally sinful for me is my *will*, my refusal to respond to God, thus consciously, deliberately setting myself in serious opposition to *His will.*

Please don't misunderstand this. This does not mean that to commit a mortal sin I need to be specifically focused on trying to set myself against God. As a matter of fact, my "hidden" and perhaps deeper sin may be that I'm not focused on God at all. I may simply be focused on something that I want to do, and ignoring God completely, conveniently pushing Him out of my mind so that I can pursue my desired agenda without guilt. As Pope John Paul II writes,

> Mortal sin exists also when a person knowingly and willingly, for whatever reason, chooses something gravely disordered. In fact, such a choice already includes contempt for the divine law, a rejection of God's love for humanity and the whole of creation.
>
> *Reconciliation and Penance, #17*

Our ability to love depends on our relationship with God. The closer my union with God, the more I am able to act like Him, to love like Him. Anytime I choose to reject God's laws, anytime I choose to do something that is not according to His will, my relationship with Him suffers because I have turned away from Him and severed myself, in varying degrees, from His goodness within me.

So, in examining the seriousness of my sin, I shouldn't just look at where this action is on a list, but rather ask myself, "To what extent have I wounded the love God put inside me? To what degree have I separated myself from right relationship with God?"

In order to determine this, I need to consider the *personal dimension of sin*, the extent to which I am culpable, guilty of consciously turning away from God.

You have probably heard the phrase "mitigating circumstances." According to Church teaching, the degree of responsibility or culpability that I bear for committing a grave offense may be "mitigated" (meaning "diminished") by various circumstances, including "unintentional ignorance, … the promptings of feelings and passions, … external pressures, … [and] pathological disorders."

So the sins for which I am most culpable are those I commit, not through weakness, but through malice, deliberately choosing evil (see *Catechism*, #1860).

What does all this mean? It means that although we can legitimately judge that a person's action is, in itself, a serious offense, we have to leave the judgment of the person to God (see *Catechism,* #1861).

When you commit an action which is, by its very nature, seriously wrong, only God can know whether you are doing it with full knowledge and complete consent. Only God can determine how completely and deliberately you are rejecting the bond of love between you and Him, and between you and other people. Only God can accurately judge whether this sin — *for you* — is mortal or venial (see *Catechism,* # 1862).

There! We are finally getting close to the theme of this chapter: your sin is different from my sin because what is a mortal sin for me may only be a venial sin for you; what is a mortal sin for you may only be a venial sin for me. We may both do the same wrong actions, but our degree of culpability for those actions may be extremely different.

God sees every big and little thought, word, and action with complete clarity. God — and only God — is aware of all the circumstances surrounding every action you commit, and He is aware of all that is in your mind and heart when you commit it. So only God can judge how guilty you are and how mortally you have sinned.

So, if only God can judge, then how can I ever determine what's right and wrong? How can I know when I need to go to confession before receiving Communion? How can I fully and accurately examine my conscience?

As I mentioned earlier, the guidelines given to us by the Church, through its teachings, through the *Catechism*, are a great place to start. But I also need to examine where I am with God on a personal level.

Perhaps an example will help. Earlier in this chapter I emphasized that our central focus must always be on our person-to-person relationship with God. So, let's look a little deeper into that.

If you woke up in the middle of the night and couldn't get back to sleep, would it be a sin not to spend that time in prayer?

Of course not! There's no commandment, no Church teaching that says you have to pray if you wake up at night. And if you were to walk into the confessional and confess that you woke up at night but didn't pray for someone, the priest would probably look at you as if you had two heads and tell you that it wasn't a sin (although I hope he would ask you some questions first).

But for me, there was a time when it would have been sin.

I had never had a problem sleeping. But at one point in my life, I began waking up every night, and I had trouble getting back to sleep. It puzzled me and bothered me, because it didn't feel like just a physical thing. I felt somehow that there was some reason for it, but I couldn't get a handle on what it was.

When I mentioned this to my spiritual director, he thought about it for a minute and then quietly asked me, "Vinny, has it occurred to you that God might be asking you to spend that time in prayer for someone?"

As soon as he asked the question, it felt right; I didn't even have to think about it. I was completely convinced that this was what was happening.

From that time on, whenever I awoke, I would begin to pray for whoever needed prayer (unknown to me, but known to God). Usually, I would fall asleep again after a short time, but then, instead of feeling irritation, I would feel a sense of peace.

If during that time, I had awakened, realized that God wanted me to pray, but refused to do so, then it would have been sin for me. Mortal? Venial? I don't know, and I don't care. It would have been a direct, conscious refusal to respond to God, and that is always sin, always unhealthy, always harmful to my relationship with God.

We need to remember that sin is not just about actions, not just about rules and regulations, and not the same for everyone. It's very personal and specific to each one's unique relationship with God. One of the lines of scripture that scares me most is this:

> Much will be required of the person entrusted with much, and still more will be demanded of the person entrusted with more.
>
> Luke 12:48

God asks — and expects — each of us to act according to the specific, unique, personal abilities, awareness, and experiences He has given us. Yes, there are certainly some common things that God asks of all of us — and so we need to observe the commandments and teachings of the Church.

But there are other things — lots of them — that God asks of me, day-by-day, that He doesn't ask of you, and other things that He asks of you but doesn't ask of me.

Imagine that you and I are playing cards. God is the dealer. He deals you a particular hand, and He deals me a different hand. He doesn't expect you to play my hand or me to play your hand. He expects each of us to play the hand we were dealt. If you received a pair of threes and I received four aces, He would expect much more from me.

For real spiritual growth into holiness, I need to develop a uniquely personal and *positive* spirituality. It's important to recognize good and evil and to struggle against any temptations or addictions that will lead to serious sins of pride, anger, lust, greed, gluttony, etc. But it's not enough to have a list of things I *shouldn't* do.

I need to go deeper. Yes, God wants me to avoid evil thoughts, words, and actions. But there are also personal and unique things He is asking me to do, moment by moment, that may be different from the things He is asking someone else to do. It's this personal dimension that is so often missing in our relationship with God.

I'm the father of seven children, and I love them all. But not just "all." I love them "each." I love them all equally, but I love each one differently. Each is a completely unique person, and if I tried to treat them all the same, it would be a disaster. So, gradually, my relationship with each one has developed into a one-on-one, personal relationship that is different from any other.

In Secret 1, I talked about how God is not just our *creator*, but our *Father*, and that you and I are not just casual or accidental creations. We were *willed* to exist, *fathered* into life. We need to really understand what this means.

You exist because God the Father wanted you as His child. Knowing in advance all the millions of different persons that could have been born from your mother and father, He chose you. He wanted you born. He loves you differently than He has ever loved anyone else, and He wants to father you, leading you on a personal journey to the holiness that will fill you with joy and enable you to be with Him forever.

Scripture makes this so clear:

> Before I formed you in the womb, I knew you (Jer 1:5). ... See, upon the palms of my hands, I have written your name (Is 43:3). ... I have loved you with an everlasting love (Jer 31:3 RSV). ... You are precious in my eyes (Is 43:4). ... Even the hairs on your head are all numbered (Mt 10:30 RSV). ... I will be a father to you (2 Cor 6:16). ... When you seek me with all your heart, you will find me with you (Jer 29:11).

With all your heart! Christ calls each of us, not merely to avoid major sin, but to seek God with all our heart. At every intersection of my life, every big and little point of decision, God the Father gives me the grace, through Christ, in the power of the Holy Spirit, to respond in accordance to His will for me at that moment. To fail to respond is sin — sin that pulls me off the personal path to holiness that He has chosen for me. It's a refusal to be fathered by God.

It comes down to this: Am I going to spend my life in a mechanical observance of "do's and don'ts," or am I going to respond to the personal love of God the Father and do whatever He calls me to do at each moment?

Imagine St. Peter greeting you at the "Pearly Gates." He pulls a large volume from the shelf and starts flipping through the pages until he comes to your name. His face lights up momentarily with an approving smile:

"Well, I see you've done a pretty good job resisting temptation and avoiding serious sin."

He turns a page, and then another, and another. "Hmmm ... " He looks up sadly: "But there's an awful lot you haven't done."

Ouch! It reminds me of the way I sometimes feel at the beginning of Mass. There's a phrase from the "Confiteor," during the penitential rite, that jumps right out and smacks me. It's the part where, along with the priest and the rest of the congregation, I confess that I have sinned "in what I have done and in what I have failed to do."

Ever think about that last line? How many times,

as we prepare for confession, do we think about the things we have failed to do? In identifying and acknowledging the wrong actions we have committed, do we also try to discover the good actions we have omitted?

"Every sin," writes Fr. David Knight, "is simply a failure to respond as we should."

It's so easy to get caught up in a "Thou shalt not" orientation, where we focus primarily on the things we should not do, trying our best to avoid evil, to refrain from thoughts, words, and deeds that are not good.

Is this wrong? Of course not. But there's a higher level of awareness, of striving, where we try to focus on what we should do, moment by moment. In other words, we don't think, "Thou shalt not ..." We think, "What would God want me to do? What can I do that would please Him?"

This is a much more personal thing, because it involves a one-on-one relationship with God, whereby I try to hear and respond, not just to an external set of rules, but to an inner awareness of what God is calling me to do at each moment.

Congratulations! You made it to the end of this chapter. This is the toughest chapter, because there's so much! Entire books have been written just on this subject alone.

The heart of it is this: We need to get beyond the commandments, beyond focusing merely on behavior to focus on our personal response to God. We need to imitate the complete devotion of Jesus, who told us "The one who sent me has not left me alone, because I always do what is pleasing to him."

Each of us is called to "always do what is pleasing" to God by responding to Him, moment-by moment, in whatever ways He is calling us to respond. Not to do so is sin.

What it comes down to is loving God and seeking Him with your whole heart — not just avoiding sin, but longing to do His will in all things.

So, yes, let's try to keep the Ten Commandments and avoid doing anything we know is wrong. But let's also keep in mind Mary's famous one-liner at Cana and let it become our guiding principle for continuous growth in personal holiness: "Do whatever he tells you" (Jn 2:5).

YOUR SIN IS DIFFERENT FROM MY SIN

$\mathscr{S}$ECRET 4

Confession is Never Really Private

When you approach the confessional, know this,
that I Myself am waiting there for you.

St. Faustina, Diary, 1602

There are a lot of misconceptions and misunder-standings that people have about the sacrament of Reconciliation, but one thing that almost everyone knows — Catholics and non-Catholics alike — is that sacramental confession is an extremely private matter between the penitent and the priest.

Over the years, there has been a lot of publicity

and discussion about the "seal" of confession, which forbids the priest to ever reveal or make use of any information he hears in the confessional. As the *Catechism* explains:

> Every priest who hears confessions is bound under very severe penalties to keep absolute secrecy regarding the sins that his penitents have confessed to him. He can make no use of knowledge that confession gives him about penitents' lives. This secret, which admits of no exceptions, is called the "sacramental seal," because what the penitent has made known to the priest remains "sealed" by the sacrament.
>
> #1467

The traditional use of a screen has served to make the conversation between priest and penitent even more private, allowing the penitent to confess without even being seen by the priest. Even after the introduction of a face-to-face option, where there is no separating screen, the penitent always has the right to choose the traditional method and thus remain "incognito."

The careful placement and construction of confessionals to ensure privacy and secrecy has always been an important consideration, and in situations where confessions are heard outside or in open areas of buildings, utmost care is taken to ensure that the penitent's confession will not be overheard by anyone else.

But in reality, confession is never really private. Though it seems to be a confidential, one-on-one conversation with the priest, there's something you should know:

There are always others listening.

I love the shocked reactions I get from people when I say this during a talk. Jaws drop, eyes widen, heads start shaking in denial. I laugh and say, "Okay, now that I have your attention, let me explain."

Talking to a priest in the confessional is not the same as talking to anyone else. The priest is still an individual human being like you and me, but he is not acting on his own. He is acting *in persona Christi* — in the person of Christ.

Archbishop José Gomez, in his pastoral letter, *The Tender Mercy of Our God*, explains:

> By his ordination, the priest is granted sacred power to share in the priesthood of Christ. The priest is anointed with the Holy Spirit and given a new and special character that enables him to act *in persona Christi Capitis* — in the person of Christ, who is the head of his Church. This means that in the confessional, the priest, by the grace of God, speaks with the very voice of Christ. What we hear in the confessional, then, are Christ's own words of healing and pardon, addressed to our individual circumstances.

As I wrote in *7 Secrets of the Eucharist*, the priest, through his ordination, "is not merely authorized to represent Christ, but rather is uniquely and sacramentally identified with Him."

So what? So it's not just the priest who hears your confession; and it's not the priest who acts in your soul. It's Christ. As Pope John Paul II explains,

> In the sacrament of Reconciliation we are all invited to meet Christ personally.

He stresses that this is why individual confession is so necessary, because it provides each of us with the opportunity for "a more personal encounter with the crucified, forgiving Christ, with Christ saying, through the minister of the sacrament, ... 'Your sins are forgiven; go and do not sin again.'"

To meet Christ personally? I was never taught that. As a child, I was taught how to go to confession, and I was taught that, if I committed serious sin, then I *had* to go to confession.

I learned all about the the ritual and the rules, but I never heard anything about going to meet Jesus personally. And yet this is the most important thing for us all to understand!

As Fr. Raniero Cantalamessa explains, we need to learn

> not to live confession as a rite, a habit, or a canonical obligation, but as a personal encounter with the Risen One who allows us, as he did Thomas, to touch his wounds, to feel in ourselves the healing force of his blood and taste the joy of being saved.

Christ made this very clear to St. Faustina:

> When you approach the confessional,
> know this, that I Myself am waiting there
> for you. I am only hidden by the priest, but
> I Myself act in your soul.
>
> *Diary* 1602

Like the Eucharist, confession is an incarnational encounter, a personal meeting with Jesus Christ, the Word made flesh. In the confessional, in a different but very real way, we come into personal contact with the same Christ we receive in the Eucharist.

In the Eucharist, Christ is present for us hidden under the appearances of bread and wine. In the confessional, Christ is hidden in the priest. Just as it is really Christ who consecrates the bread and wine through the words of the priest, so it is Christ who absolves us of our sins through the words of the priest.

> You make your confession before me.
> The person of the priest is, for Me, only a
> screen.
> Never analyze what sort of a priest it is
> that I am making use of; open your soul in

confession as you would to Me, and I will fill it with My light."

Diary 1725

So, you are never really alone with the priest. Christ is present, too.

If you're thinking, "Yes, of course! I know that," guess what? He's not really alone either. Christ is never alone. Wherever Christ is, the Father is and the Holy Spirit is, because the three persons of the Trinity cannot be separated.

In *7 Secrets of the Eucharist*, I devote a whole chapter to this truth, so let it suffice here to offer a few brief passages from the *Catechism*:

> The Trinity is One. We do not confess three Gods, but one God in three persons. … The whole Christian life is a communion with each of the divine persons, without in any way separating them.
>
> #253, 259, 260

If our hearts are right, we not only experience Christ in the person of the priest, but we receive in

the confessional what we receive in the Eucharist —
the very life of the Triune God. It's a very real reception of spiritual communion. We receive the Three
Divine Persons, who come to dwell in our hearts.

St. Faustina writes:

> When I left the confessional ... God's
> presence penetrated me and ... I felt, or
> rather, discerned, the Three Divine Persons
> dwelling in me.
>
> *Diary* 175

> Earlier in the *Diary* , she had said the
> same thing about receiving Communion:

> In the morning, after Holy Com-
> munion, my soul was immersed in the
> Godhead. I was united to the Three Divine
> Persons in such a way that when I was
> united to Jesus, I was simultaneously united
> to the Father and to the Holy Spirit.
>
> 1073

As the *Catechism* summarizes it:

> The ultimate end of the whole divine

economy is the entry of God's creatures into the perfect unity of the Blessed Trinity. But even now we are called to be a dwelling place for the Most Holy Trinity.

#260

Remember what I shared in the Foreword about how I used to feel so differently about confession and Communion? Anytime I'd realize I had serious sin on my soul, I'd think, "I *want* to go to Communion, so now I *have* to go to confession."

How silly that seems now:

> "Oh, no! I've sinned, so now I *have* to go for a personal, healing encounter with the Trinity — to be cleansed and healed and forgiven, embraced by the tender love of the Father, the Son, and the Holy Spirit."

"*Have* to go?" I don't *have* to go. I *get* to go! It's a gift, an incredible gift! And, if I'm open to receive it, it will fill me with new joy, new hope, new life, new purpose, new awareness of how loved I am by God.

It's no accident that in the Formula for

Absolution that is proclaimed by the priest in the confessional, the Trinity is mentioned twice, emphasizing how God the Father, by sending us, first Jesus, and then the Holy Spirit, is drawing us back to Himself:

> God the Father of mercies, through the death and resurrection of his Son has reconciled the world to himself and sent the Holy Spirit among us for the forgiveness of sins; through the ministry of the Church may God give you pardon and peace, and I absolve you from your sins in the name of the Father and of the Son and of the Holy Spirit.
>
> *Catechism,* #1449

Pope John Paul II makes it unmistakably clear that at this moment of absolution the Holy Trinity actually becomes present:

> The sacramental formula "I absolve you" and the imposition of the hand and the Sign of the Cross made over the penitent show that at this moment the contrite and converted sinner comes into contact with the power and mercy of God. It is the

moment at which, in response to the penitent, *the Trinity becomes present* to blot out sin and restore innocence.

Reconciliation and Penance, #31

The *Catechism* also references the absolution formula of the Byzantine Liturgy, which speaks of the sacrament of Reconciliation's power to enable us to appear before God's "awe-inspiring tribunal without condemnation" (#1481).

In the *Diary of St. Faustina*, we hear Jesus using a similar phrase, referring to confession as a "Tribunal of Mercy" (1448).

"Tribunal of Mercy?" The words seem almost contradictory, like "hot ice." The word *tribunal* seems to suggest a judicial court that administers justice, while *mercy* suggests tender love and forgiveness.

Pope John Paul II uses exactly the same phrase Christ had used to St. Faustina:

> The sacrament is a kind of "judicial action"; but this takes place before a tribunal of mercy rather than of strict and rigorous justice.
>
> *Reconciliation and Penance, #31*

Let's take a closer look at this word *tribunal*. The prefix *tri*, of course, means three, so the word is normally understood as referring to a court presided over by three judges.

The word is from the Latin *tribunus*, and refers primarily to the office of tribune, established in the Roman Republic roughly 500 years before Christ, as a protection for the common people to insure that they received justice.

If a magistrate, or an assembly, or even the senate itself took action against any Roman citizen, the citizen could appeal to the tribune, who had the power to veto any government action. The tribunes were advocates for the common people, and were really their only representatives.

In confession, through the ministry of the priest acting *in persona Christi*, we are brought into the presence of God's "awe-inspiring tribunal" — the Tribunal of Mercy: the Father, the Son, and the Holy Spirit. But they aren't there to sit in judgment. They're on our side.

We need to understand that we're not dealing with abstract concepts here. What we're dealing with is *persons* — divine, yes, but *real persons*, each distinct from the other, yet inseparable! Jesus is a person; the Holy Spirit is a person; the Father is a person. And together these three persons of God have one goal: to bring us back to the Father, the source of all life, all goodness, all blessing.

"Reconciliation," writes Pope John Paul II, "is principally a gift of the heavenly Father."

This, to me, is the most important thing, and it's something I never knew:

Confession is all about the Father.

In the confessional, Christ, through the power of the Holy Spirit, leads us back to the Father so that, now that we have been "ransomed, healed, restored, and forgiven," we can enter into the fullness of our dignity as His children.

Pope Benedict XVI points out that the role of priests in the confessional is "to make their penitents experience the Heavenly Father's merciful love," because what is central to confession is the "personal encounter with God, the Father of goodness and mercy."

The "call to conversion," he explains, is

> an encouragement to return to the arms of
> God, the tender and merciful Father, to
> trust in him and to entrust ourselves to him
> as his adopted children, regenerated by his
> love. ... To convert means to let Jesus con-
> quer our hearts ... and "to return" with him
> to the Father.

If only we could really understand the infinite love
and tenderness of this Father who waits for us to
come to Him in the confessional! Comparing God
the Father to the father of the prodigal son, Pope
John Paul II writes:

> Did not Christ say that our Father, who
> "sees in secret," is always waiting for us to
> have recourse to Him in every need and
> always waiting for us to study His mystery:
> the mystery of the Father and His love?
>
> *Rich in Mercy, #2*

To have recourse to Him in every need! God is a perfect Father. How does any good father react when
one of his children is hurt or in trouble and needs

help? Imagine a little toddler who falls and hurts herself and runs to her daddy. Would he hold her off at a distance and say, "Sorry, no blood, no band-aid"? Or would he hug her close, ask where it hurts, and kiss her to make it better?

Archbishop Gomez writes that this hug, this embrace of a loving Father, is what we receive in the confessional:

> In going to confession, we are like the prodigal son, finally aware of our sinfulness, responding to the call of our conscience, arising and going to our Father. Through the sacred ministry of the priest in the confessional, the Father in his compassion stretches out his arms to welcome and embrace us.

Confession is not just admitting your sins in a private conversation with a priest. It's when a child who has fallen and hurt himself runs to His father to make it all better. Confession is running to Daddy!

But wait ... there's more! There are still others involved.

In chapter 15 of St. Luke's Gospel, just before the parable of the prodigal son, Jesus relates two other parables of mercy. In the first, a shepherd, having somehow lost one of the hundred sheep in his care, leaves the ninety-nine others and goes in search of the lost one. When he finds it, he places it on his shoulders and carries it home, rejoicing — obviously a figure of Christ, the Good Shepherd, who goes in search of each us when we are lost in sin, and rejoices as He brings us back to the Father.

In the second parable, a woman has lost one of her ten coins. Like the shepherd, she searches desperately for it and rejoices when she finds it.

In each of these three stories, there's an important teaching that can easily go unnoticed — a teaching most powerfully expressed in the parable of the prodigal son.

The father in the parable rejoices at the return of his son, but he does not rejoice alone. In great haste, he calls upon his servants to prepare a special feast so that all may share his joy:

Quickly bring the finest robe and put it

on him; put a ring on his finger and sandals on his feet. Take the fattened calf and slaughter it. Then let us celebrate with a feast, because this son of mine was dead, and has come to life again; he was lost, and has been found.

Luke 15: 22-24

In a similar way, the shepherd and the woman with the coins each immediately call upon others to share their joy that what was lost has now been found. The shepherd

calls together his friends and neighbors and says to them, "Rejoice with me because I have found my lost sheep."

Luke 15:6

And the woman who had found the lost coin

calls together her friends and neighbors and says to them, "Rejoice with me because I have found the coin that I lost."

Luke 15:9

What's the message here? We need to make the jump from earth to heaven, recognizing that, like the main characters in the three parables, our heavenly Father is not content to rejoice alone, but wants to share His joy each time one of His lost children has been found.

But share it with whom? Who's doing all this rejoicing? Who are God's "servants," "friends," and "neighbors"? Jesus gives us the answer in each of the first two parables. As the shepherd calls on his friends to rejoice, Jesus tells us,

> I tell you, in just the same way there will be more joy in heaven over one sinner who repents than over ninety-nine righteous people who have no need of repentance.
>
> Luke 15: 7

And again, as the woman rejoices with her friends,

> In just the same way, I tell you, there will be rejoicing among the angels of God over one sinner who repents.
>
> Luke 15:10

In the confessional, God the Father, together with Jesus and the Holy Spirit, is filled with joy as you return to Him, and He immediately shares that joy with all those who are in perpetual union with Him in heaven.

Your reception of the sacrament is not a private, isolated experience, but has immediate repercussions "in the presence of the angels." At your repentance, your acknowledgment of God's mercy, your sincere confession of sin, your acts of penance, and your resolution to avoid further sin — *all of heaven rejoices.*

There is yet another way in which confession is never a completely private matter — because it involves sin.

In one sense, sin is always a personal act and has personal consequences. But we need to understand that none of us exists in a vacuum. We each live in the world and are inextricably bound together in an interconnected relationship with that world and with each other.

I remember when, as a teenager beginning my first courses in philosophy, I was introduced to the concept that, because everything is so interconnected, every action — no matter how small — has a positive or negative effect on the universe.

One of the examples that was given concerned the "ripple effect" of our actions in the physical world. If you throw a stone into a quiet pond, you create ripples that spread throughout the water and in some way affect the entire pond and everything in it.

Some of this we can actually see, as the calm surface of the water is shattered, and the repercussions are visible in the initial splash and the concentric circles that spread outward from the point of impact. But there are hidden effects as well, which can only be discerned through scientific observation and measurement.

Though not as easily measured, the same concept holds true in the spiritual realm — and the stone is sin. As Pope John Paul II writes,

> Man's rupture with God leads tragically to divisions between brothers. ... The result of sin is the shattering of the human family.
>
> *Reconciliation and Penance*, #15

Sin ... is always a personal act ... [but]

each individual's sin in some way affects others. ... There is no sin, not even the most intimate and secret one, ... that exclusively concerns the person committing it. ... Every sin has repercussions on the entire ecclesial body [the Church] and the whole human family.

Reconciliation and Penance, #16

As Archbishop Gomez explains, these repercussions on the Church and the world occur because, when you and I reject God through sin, we are also rejecting each other:

When we sin, we "disown" God as our Father, we reject our relationship as his sons and daughters. ... We also injure our fellowship with others, because in denying God's fatherhood, in effect we deny that we are sisters and brothers to each other. This is why our personal sins always have consequences in society. ... There is no sin that is "victimless" or private. We are bound to each other by our common humanity, and when we sin we weaken these bonds.

Since your sin — your rejection of God —affects

me, and mine affects you, the same is true of our confession. What happens in the confessional — reconciliation, healing, restoration — is not just a private matter between you and God.

Since your sins, first and foremost, have weakened and wounded your relationship with God, the healing of that wound and the restoration of your friendship with Him is, of course, the first reconciliation that takes place.

But the *Catechism* identifies four other wounds or rifts that are also repaired in the confessional — wounds to yourself, to others, to the Church, and to all creation:

> This reconciliation with God leads … to other reconciliations, which repair the other breeches caused by sin. The forgiven penitent is reconciled with *himself* in his inmost being, … He is reconciled with his *brethren* whom he has in some way offended and wounded. He is reconciled with the *Church*. He is reconciled with all *creation*.
>
> #1469

So confession is not only my personal, one-to-One

restoration of communion with God. In each individual experience of this sacrament, God, in Christ — and through the Church — is "reconciling the world to himself" (2 Cor 5:19) and fulfilling the priestly prayer of Christ:

> … that they may be one, as you, Father, are in me and I am in you … that they may be one, as we are one, I in them and you in me, that they may become completely one.
>
> John 17:21-23 NRSV

$\mathcal{S}$ECRET 5
You've Got Mail!

*When you go to confession, ... the Blood and Water
which came forth from My Heart always flows
down upon your soul and ennobles it.*

Jesus to St. Faustina, *Diary, 1602*

When you decide to go to confession, there are a lot of things to think about. What sins have I committed? In what areas of my life am I struggling? How should I explain things to the priest? How is he going to react?

Once you enter the confessional, there's a lot to

do. You confess your sins to the priest, talk with him, listen to him, pray an act of contrition, accept your penance, and finally receive absolution.

It's a very focused process, and the various stages and actions of the ritual itself are so specific, so personal, so momentous that it's easy to view confession as an isolated event.

But it's not. All the rituals of the Church are connected. All came from the Father and lead back to the Father. All are linked to the saving action of Jesus as, in the power of the Holy Spirit, He fulfills the Father's plan of mercy for all.

Confession takes us to the Cross.

This is not just a pious phrase, not just symbolic, not just a remembering of the crucifixion. Confession actually brings us to Calvary. As Pope Benedict XVI points out:

> The Way of the Cross is not something of the past and of a specific point on earth. The Lord's cross embraces the world, his Way of the Cross goes across continents

and time. We cannot just be spectators on the Way of the Cross. We are involved.

In my earlier book, *7 Secrets of the Eucharist*, in the chapter entitled "There is only one Mass," I interrupt myself to give a little "science lesson" about time. I need to do that here, too, because the Mass and Confession are inseparably linked, to each other and to the cross, and there's no way you can understand that if you don't know what time is for God.

You see, you and I — because we are so limited by time and space — tend to look at the crucifixion as a single event that happened at a specific time (about 2,000 years ago) and in a specific place (the hill of Calvary outside Jerusalem).

We may think about it, be grateful for it, try to learn from it, but we view it as simply an historic event. It began at a specific moment; it ended at a specific moment; and now it's over and done with.

But it's not! To God,

> One day is like a thousand years, and a thousand years like one day.
>
> 2 Peter 3:8

As the *Catechism* explains, "To God, all moments of time are present in their immediency (#600). Unlike us, God is not limited by time and space. He sees everything — past, present, and future — all at once. For God, everything is always present; God lives in the *Eternal Now*.

The Church teaches that Christ's suffering, death, resurrection, and ascension are not separate events. They form one, unique event — the paschal mystery — which cannot be assigned to any specific time or place. It is never over.

The *Catechism* explains that the paschal mystery is different from every other historical event because they all happen once and then end. They all "pass away, swallowed up in the past." But the paschal mystery "cannot remain only in the past." It is "the unique event of history which does not pass away":

> All that Christ is — all that He did and suffered for men — participates in the divine eternity, and so transcends all times while being present in them all. The event of the Cross and Resurrection abides and draws everything toward life.
>
> #1084

Pretty amazing! These dramatic events of Christ's passion, death, and resurrection — which actually took place, here on earth, in the "fullness of time" — are so linked to God's life in the Eternal Now, that they are *timeless*! They never end!

How does this relate to the Mass and confession? In his encyclical letter on the Eucharist, Pope John Paul II writes that all the fruits of Christ's passion, death, and resurrection are "concentrated forever in the gift of the Eucharist."

He goes on to explain that, in this gift of the Eucharist, Christ entrusted to the Church the "perennial making present" of the paschal mystery, and so effected a "oneness of time." The Eucharist "applies to men and women today the reconcilation won by Christ for mankind in every age."

Is your head spinning yet? "Perennial making present"? … "oneness of time"? … "applies today"? What does all that mean?

It means that each time you participate in the Mass, each time you receive the Eucharist, each moment you spend in Eucharistic Adoration, all that Christ won for you 2,000 years ago on the cross at

Calvary is applied to you *now* in your present moment and present place.

Take a minute and let that really sink in. Through this "oneness of time," what He did *then* affects you *now*. You are at the cross with Mary and John, and the blood and water from Christ's pierced Heart is gushing forth upon you as a fountain of mercy.

What about confession? The same thing happens. Time and space disappear, and you are at Calvary 2,000 years ago. As Our Lord revealed to St. Faustina:

> **When you go to confession, to this fountain of My mercy, the Blood and Water which came forth from My Heart always flows down upon your soul and ennobles it.**
>
> *Diary*, 1602

It's so important to understand how connected the sacraments of Eucharist and Reconciliation are. As Pope John Paul II pointed out, both sacraments were instituted in the same room (the Cenacle); and the institution of the sacrament of Reconciliation immediately after Christ's passion and death, on the very day of the Resurrection, is so significant that it "should be considered alongside the importance of the Eucharist itself."

In the *Diary of St. Faustina*, when you come across words like "Miracle of Mercy" … "Fountain of Life" … "Fountain of Mercy," you need to check the context in order to determine whether the Lord is speaking about Eucharist or Reconciliation, because He uses the same phrases for each.

We, on the other hand, tend to refer to the two sacraments differently, and the words we use for each can limit our understanding of how related they are. We say that we "receive" Communion, but we "go" to confession.

Well, as I mentioned in Secret 2, in the confessional we also receive. Through our sincere confession and the absolution of the priest, we experience a spiritual and very real communion with the three divine persons who come to dwell in our hearts.

How does this happen? The same way it happens when we receive the Eucharist: the fruits that Christ won for us on the cross are applied to us *now* in the confessional through this "oneness of time."

Everything comes from the cross!

A couple of years ago, during a celebration of the Exaltation of the Cross, I had an experience that brought this realization home to me in an extremely personal way.

When it came time for the veneration of the cross, I walked up with the others in the congregation, bent down to kiss the foot of the cross, and then started to walk away.

But the priest suddenly reached out and grabbed my arm to hold me in place and, with his other hand, he pressed the cross against my heart and held it there for what seemed like a long time. I have no idea why he did it — maybe I just looked so bad that he figured I needed a special blessing. But whatever the reason, it had a very powerful effect on me, and I found myself praying silently, over and over, "Lord, I receive your love from the cross."

The next morning, when I went up to receive Communion, the same prayer came to me: "Lord, I receive your love from the cross." And now, when I go to confession, it's the same prayer. "Lord, I receive your love from the cross."

It all comes from the cross.

In Secret 2, I mentioned that, when we think about confession, we often focus too much on forgiveness without realizing how much more there is to this sacrament. But even the reality of forgiveness itself has to be understood from the perspective of the Eternal Now.

I remember how often I used to go to confession kind of cringing inside, almost afraid to dare to ask for forgiveness. I was so cowed spiritually: "Oh, please God, I know I don't deserve it, but please forgive me." It was as if I thought He might not forgive me, as if I were trying to wring forgiveness out of Him.

How silly! Christ isn't forgiving me now in the confessional. He forgave me 2,000 years ago! I'm just *receiving* it now.

We need to remember that Christ on the cross is God! He is the God-Man. So He is not limited by time or space as we are. The *Catechism* is so clear and so specific about this:

> Jesus knew and loved us each and all during his life, his agony and his Passion, and gave himself up for each one of us.
>
> #478

Read that again and think about it. All during Christ's life, all during His agony, all during His Passion, Christ knew and loved *you!* He gave Himself up and died for you. If you had been the only human being who needed to be saved, Christ would have died just for you. That's how precious each individual person is to God.

You weren't even born yet. Your parents and grandparents weren't even born yet. But Christ isn't subject to time. He saw you, knew you, loved you, and died for you on the cross.

Why? Why did He allow Himself to die? What did His death accomplish?

Forgiveness. The forgiveness of sin — all sin. Your sins, my sins, and all the sins of the whole world, from the beginning to the end of time.

St. Paul teaches that Christ took on all our sins, so much so that it was as though God made Him to *be* sin for our sake (see 2 Cor 5:21).

From the cross, Christ reached across 2,000 years of time and space, saw you, saw all your sin (past sin, present sin, future sin) — and loved you!

He pulled all your sin, all my sin — all that awful stuff — into His pure body, and when His body was destroyed on the cross, our sin was destroyed, too.

It's a done deal. He "bore our sins in his body upon the cross" (1 Pet 2:24), and died "once, for all" (Rom 6:10).

I said our sin was "destroyed." This is really important to understand, but a lot of people miss it. At Mass, we don't say, "Lamb of God, you forgive the sins of the world"; we say, "Lamb of God, you take away the sins of the world." Christ doesn't just *forgive* our sins; He *takes them away!*

Scripture tell us, "As far as the east is from the west, so far does he remove our sins" (Ps 103:12). And again, "It is I who *wipe out* ... your offenses. Your sins I remember no more" (Is 44:25).

Yet so many people have told me that the memories of past sins keep coming back to haunt them — even though they've already confessed them — and they wonder whether they've really been forgiven.

Don't ever let yourself doubt God's mercy! If you have sincerely repented of your sins, confessed them, resolved not to repeat them, and received absolution, then they're not just forgiven; *they're gone!*

And it doesn't matter how bad your sins were. No sin is greater than God's love:

> Though your sins be like scarlet,
> they may become white as snow.
>
> Isaiah 1:18

In the *Diary* of St. Faustina, there's a beautiful conversation between Christ and a despairing soul, which is so horrified at the thought of its sins that it doubts that God could forgive it.

Jesus tells the soul:

> **All your sins have not wounded my heart as painfully as your present lack of trust does — that after so many efforts of My love and mercy, you should still doubt My goodness.**
>
> 1486

The soul begins to reply, but Jesus, seeing its turmoil, interrupts, raises it up, and "leads it into the recesses of His Heart, where all its sins *disappear* instantly" (1486). This is the power of Christ's mercy from the cross.

For my *Endless Mercy* CD, I wrote a song to express how personal and complete this saving action on the cross was:

> From the cross, you saw my sin
> and loved me.
> You felt my pain
> and reached through time to heal me.
> With gentle hands
> you pulled my sin into yourself,
> and by your death
> destroyed it all forever.

When we enter the confessional, we shouldn't go with the idea that we need to *beg* Christ to forgive us. Yes, we ask for forgiveness, but we do so with expectant and grateful faith, knowing that Christ already won it for us on the cross, even though we didn't deserve it, and that He is simply waiting for us to ask for it, so that we can receive it into our lives now.

When I speak about this at events or parish missions, I have two favorite comparisons I like to give to help make all this really clear.

The first is for those of you who use email. I remember when I first began to go online to send and receive email. My brother sent me an email message from Japan.

I was traveling at the time and didn't have a computer with me, so it was a couple of weeks before I got home, went online, and discovered that he had sent me a note.

I remember thinking, "How amazing! He sent this to me from halfway across the world two weeks ago, but I didn't know it, so I'm only getting it now. It's just been sitting there somewhere in cyberspace waiting for me."

Two thousand years ago, Jesus Christ, from the cross, emailed you all the forgiveness and healing you will ever need. Do you have it? No. It's floating around in spiritual cyberspace waiting for you. It's there for you, but you have to *do* something to get it. As St. Augustine said, "God created us without us: but He did not will to save us without us." We need to participate in the process.

What do you need to do to get your email? You need to turn on your computer, open your browser, and log on to your email account with your screen name and password. Then you hear: "You've got mail!" Now you can click on the file, read it, print it, download it, use it. It's yours now.

Confession is logging on. It's doing the things you need to do now so that you can access what Christ did for you then. It allows you to download into your life all the fruits of Christ's Passion, death, and resurrection right now in your present moment of need.

Just like the celebration of the Eucharist, confession is the *now* reception of a *then* gift.

The second comparison is for anyone who is not familiar with email. Two thousand years ago, Christ put all the forgiveness and healing you will ever need into a safe deposit box in your name, and He gave you the key.

It's there waiting for you, but you need to do something to get it. You need to go to the bank, show your identification, get one of the attendants to bring the matching key, and then go open the box. Now you have it.

Understanding all this can help make confession a much richer experience. But so far, I've only given you half of the story of the Eternal Now. Everything I've told you relates to the reality that what Christ did *then* affects us *now*.

But it works the other way around, too. What you and I do *now* affected Him *then*.

When I was a sophomore in high school, I read a poem that moved me so deeply that I memorized it, and it still helps me remember how present the cross always is for us:

Why the Robin's Breast is Red

The Saviour, bowed beneath his cross,
climbed up the dreary hill,
While from the agonizing wreath ran
many a crimson rill;
The cruel Roman thrust him on with
unrelenting hand,
'Til, staggering slowly mid the crowd,
He fell upon the sand.

A little bird that warbled near, that
memorable day

    Flitted around and strove to wrench one
single thorn away;
    The cruel spike impaled his breast,—
and thus, 'tis sweetly said,
    The Robin has his silver vest incar-
nadined with red.

    Ah, Jesu! Jesu! Son of man! My dolor
and my sighs,
    Reveal the lesson taught by this winged
Ishmael of the skies.
    I, in my palace of delight or cavern of
despair,
    Have plucked no thorns from thy dear
brow, but planted thousands there.

s

At each moment of each day, you and I can
choose to be either the cruel Roman or the robin. We
can comfort and console Christ on the cross, or we
can add to His pain. We can pluck a thorn from His
brow or push another in. Each time I sin, I hurt Him;
and every time I do something good, I comfort Him.

This is why the best way to prepare for confession
is to stir up the "tears of repentance" by meditating on
the Passion of Christ (see *Catechism*, #1429).

A portion of the agony that Christ felt in the Garden — so intense that He sweat blood — came from seeing my sins and taking them into Himself. He was scourged, beaten, mocked, and tortured on the cross for *my* sins.

I spat on His face; *I* slapped Him; *I* tore the flesh from His body with those awful whips; *I* beat the thorns into His head; *I* nailed His hands and feet; *I* gave Him bitter gall to drink.

Sin is *personal!* It hurts a *person!* — the person who is the most undeserving of it, the most gentle, the most loving. Sin is horrible!

St. Faustina writes:

> Today, I entered into the bitterness of the Passion of the Lord Jesus. ... I learned in the depths of my soul how horrible sin was, even the smallest sin, and how much it tormented the soul of Jesus. ... O my Jesus, I would rather be in agony until the end of the world, amidst the greatest sufferings, than offend You by the least sin. ... My Jesus, I would rather not exist than make You sad.
>
> *Diary* , 1016, 741, 571

In confession we receive, but we also give. When I swallow my pride, overcome my fear, and make a sincere confession, repenting of my sins and resolving to change my life, then I console Christ on the cross.

In confession we receive the loving email of Christ, and we send a reply back to Him:

> *I'm sorry, Lord, for all the ways and times I have hurt You. Thank You for loving me anyway. Help me to love You more.*

$\mathscr{S}$ECRET 6
New Wine Needs New Skins

You should put away the old self
of your former way of life, ...
be renewed in the spirit of your minds,
and put on the new self

Ephesians 4:22-24

I'm almost afraid to start this chapter, because it's so important. Everything I've said so far — all the ideas and concepts I've shared in Secrets 1-5 — have been in preparation for this.

If you were to stop reading now, you might

just miss the whole point of it all.

All those "different" ideas are not really separate and unrelated. They are individual but connected parts of a more complete truth.

It's like a jigsaw puzzle, with a thousand little pieces spread out on a table. If you focus only on the individual pieces, you'll never finish the puzzle. You have to look for where and how the pieces are connected, so you can begin to see the picture they form together — the jigsaw puzzle of God's love.

What's the picture? It's the image of a three-personed God who fathered you into life, loves you with an everlasting love, waits with open arms for you to return every time you stray, and is always ready to forgive and heal — *so that He can recreate you and restore you to the fullness of life for which He created you in the first place.*

> I have come that they may have life and
> have it to the full.
>
> John 10:10 (NIV)

The goal of confession is new life, rebirth,

transformation, restoration of friendship, and communion with God, so that you can begin living *in a whole new way,* the way Christ Himself lives.

Ring out the old, ring in the new!

Let's take another quick look at some of the "pieces" of this confession puzzle to see how they fit together to bring about this new life.

In Secret 1, we saw that sin isn't just about behavior; it's about relationship with God. It's when we refuse to let God father us, refuse to live in right relationship with Him as His sons and daughters. We saw that our sin doesn't change God; it changes *us* by separating us from His love.

So, the real problem is not our sinful behaviors. The real problem is in our hearts. We have turned our hearts away from God. Sin has changed us; we need to let grace change us back.

Confession calls us to repentance and conversion. It calls us to do a complete about-face in the way we live: to turn our hearts back to God and come out of the cave into the light and warmth of His love.

> As your hearts have been disposed to stray from God, turn now ten times more to seek him.
>
> Baruch 4:28

Secret 2 took us a bit further. We saw that, since our sins themselves aren't the real problem, then forgiveness alone isn't the solution. We can't just confess our sinful behaviors, receive absolution, and then go back to life as usual. Our sins wound us and, even after they are forgiven, we remain wounded, confused, and spiritually weak.

We saw that forgiveness is simply the first step in a whole process of healing and holiness through grace — which is God's own way of living poured into our hearts *so that we can become like Him.*

In Secret 3, we saw that each of us is called to a personal, one-on-one relationship with God, that the call to each of us is different, and that a mere mechanical observance of "do's and don'ts" is not enough.

Confession calls us to *a change in attitude.* It calls us to seek God with all our heart, to live our lives in such a way that we try always to do what will please

Him, responding to Him, moment-by-moment by doing whatever He tells us.

In Secret 4, we saw that the confessional is a meeting place where we personally encounter the Trinity as all of heaven looks on and rejoices. Why all the rejoicing? *Because of our repentance, our conversion of heart, and our resolution to change our lives.*

In this personal meeting with the Trinity, our inner change of mind and heart allows Christ, through the power of the Holy Spirit, to lead us back to the Father so that we can be restored to our full dignity as His children.

In Secret 5, we saw that the best way to come to this necessary conversion of heart is to stir up the "tears of repentance" by meditating on the passion of Christ, entering into the reality that sin is personal, the reality that Christ suffered and died on the cross for me, personally.

And so, since Christ lives in the Eternal Now, the way I live my day-to-day life either comforts Him or adds to His pain.

What's the common denominator in all this? *Change* — change of heart and mind.

> Do not conform yourself to this age, but be transformed by the renewal of your mind.
>
> Romans 12:2

Confession, like Communion, is not just a ritual; it's not just something Catholics do; it's not just about receiving grace. It's about responding to God in such a way that our lives are *dramatically changed*.

> No one pours new wine into old wineskins. Otherwise, the wine will burst the skins, and both the wine and the skins are ruined. Rather, new wine is poured into fresh wineskins.
>
> Mark 2:22

Christ is pouring His own life into us, His own holiness. He is the "new wine," and we must receive Him in "new skins."

How do we do this? The *Catechism* presents us with three necessary steps: repentance, confessing our sins to the priest, and the intention to make reparation (see #1491).

The Act of Contrition that most Catholics used

to memorize as children provides us with a great little outline for understanding this:

> O my God, I am heartily sorry
> for having offended You ...

"I am *heartily* sorry ..." This is not an apology, not just regret for having done something stupid. The sorrow we should feel as we approach the sacrament of Confession comes from sincere repentance and conversion, "the movement of a contrite heart moved by grace *to respond to the mercy of God who loved us first*" (*Catechism,* # 1428).

Pope John Paul II explains that this conversion always consists in discovering the merciful love of the Father that Christ came to reveal. "Conversion to God," he writes, "is always the fruit of the 'rediscovery' of this Father who is rich in mercy" (*Rich in Mercy,* #13).

We see this in the case of St. Peter who, after publicly denying Christ three times, is converted by the way Christ looks at him. As the *Catechism* explains, "Jesus' look of infinite mercy drew tears of repentance from Peter and, after the Lord's resurrection, a three-fold affirmation of love for Him" (#1429).

This repentance (also known as contrition) results not only in sorrow for our sins, but also a hatred of sin:

> *and I detest all my sins, because I dread*
> *the loss of heaven, and the pains of hell.*

This first level of contrition is a contrition of fear. It's called "imperfect contrition" or "attrition," because it's motivated by an awareness of the ugliness of sin and by fear of eternal damnation. Prompted by the Holy Spirit, it begins a process of inner conversion that disposes us to grace and is completed by sacramental absolution (see *Catechism*, # 1453).

Is this enough for a valid confession? Yes, but for real growth in holiness we should try to reach a higher level:

> *but most of all because they offend You,*
> *my God, Who are all good and*
> *deserving of all my love.*

This is the second level of contrition, called "perfect contrition," motivated not by a self-oriented fear, but by love for God and the awareness of how good He is. This is much more personal, leading to a deeper relationship with God and a growing desire to avoid anything that might offend Him.

It's really just a matter of focus. If you're sorry for your sins because you're afraid of the consequences, then who are you focused on? Who do you love? Yourself. If you're sorry because you've hurt God, who are you focused on? Who do you love? God.

I firmly resolve …

These are perhaps the most important three words of our little prayer, but they are the ones most often overlooked. If sin, to me, is just bad bahavior, and if going to confession is just about having my sins forgiven so I can go to Communion, then the sacrament can all too easily become a kind of mind-less, mechanical observance, in which I simply con-fess my bad behaviors and receive absolution.

Confessing my sins is not enough; I need to make a *firm resolution* to change.

with the help of Your grace ...

Another easily overlooked phrase. If I try to fulfil this resolution on my own, I will fail. As we've seen, confession is not just about forgiveness. It's about receiving the grace we need to come to full healing and to change our lives. So, in my act of contrition before receiving absolution, I need to resolve to change, *asking for God's grace,* and depending on it. In this firm resolution, I commit to doing three things:

to confess my sins ...

But, wait a minute. By the time you say the Act of Contrition, you've *already* confessed your sins to the priest. So why does the Act of Contrition specify this as the first resolution you need to make?

Because you are resolving to say a complete yes to a *process*, not just a one-time event. You are resolving to come back to God through this sacrament every time you stray from Him through sin. You are resoving to confess your sins *regularly*.

to do penance ...

Oh, yeah, penance. That's the punishment the priest gives you because you've been bad, right?

Wrong. This is one of the most misunderstood aspects of the sacrament of Reconciliation. I remember so many times when, after receiving absolution, I'd breathe a sigh of relief:

"Whew! Thank God that's over. Now I just have to do my penance — just have to pay my dues."

But it's not over! It's just beginning — again. And penance is not a punishment or a payment. As Pope John Paul II writes, the acts of penance that we do are not a price that we pay for forgiveness. No human acts can match the value of what we obtain in the confessional.

Our penances are a sign of our

> personal commitment ... to begin a new life (and therefore they should not be reduced to mere formulas to be recited, but should consist of acts of worship, charity, mercy or reparation).
>
> *Reconciliation and Penance*, #4

He goes on to explain that, through these acts, we

join our own physical and spiritual mortification to the Passion of Christ — the one who really "paid the price" and obtained forgiveness for us.

You and I can't really "expiate" or "make up for" our sins. As we saw earlier, Christ already did that for us on the cross. We are simply offering our sacrifices to the Father, joined to Christ's "once-for-all" sacrifice so that we can become like Him.

> Such penances help configure us to Christ, who alone expiated our sins once for all. They allow us to become co-heirs with the risen Christ, "provided we suffer with him" [Rom 8:17].
>
> *Catechism*, #1460

Back to the idea of confession as a process rather than a one-time fix. We saw in Secret 2 that confession is not just about forgiveness; it's about healing. But full health doesn't come just from confessing our sins and being sorry for them. And it doesn't come just from absolution, as if the priest were waving some magic wand, and "Poof," we're healed.

> Absolution takes away sin, but it does not remedy all the disorders sin has caused.

> Raised up from sin, the sinner must still recover his full spiritual health by doing something more.
>
> *Catechism*, #1459

Pope John Paul II echoes this in his apostolic letter *Reconciliation and Penance*:

> Even after absolution there remains ... a dark area due to the wound of sin, to the imperfection of love in repentance, to the weakening of the spiritual faculties. It is an area in which there still operates an infectious source of sin which must always be fought with mortification and penance.
>
> #4

What does this all come down to? Penance isn't just doing the specific actions assigned by the priest. It's a response to the experience of God's mercy. It's a *decision*, and an *attitude* that expresses itself in real behavioral changes you make in your life, changes that bring you into fuller health and maturity as a child of God.

The penances we receive in the confessional and the absolution given by the priest are not an ending, but a "sending forth," just like the dismissal at Mass:

"Go in peace, glorifying the Lord by your life."

We express this understanding — and commit to it — in the third resolution of the Act of Contrition:

and to amend my life. Amen.

How are we called to amend our lives? Totally. Radically. The *Catechism* states this so strongly! The interior repentance that Christ is calling for in the confessional

> is a *radical reorientation* of our *whole life*, a return, a conversion to God *with all our heart*, an end of sin, a turning away from evil, with repugnance toward the evil actions we have committed. ... It entails the *desire and resolution to change one's life.*
>
> #1431

Wow! When you go to confession, do you go with the intention of radically reorienting *your whole life*? Of turning back to God *with all your heart*? Of putting *an end to sin* and turning away from *everything* that is wrong? Are you resolving to *change your life*? Or are you just rattling off some bad behaviors so they can be forgiven?

Confessing my sins is not enough. Forgiveness is not enough. I need to abandon sin. I need to restore to God what I have deprived Him of —a loving response to His love. God is calling us to respond to His love with our whole being, so that He can change our hearts and make them like His:

> *Go, and sin no more. ... Love as I have loved you. ... Forgive as you have been forgiven. ... Be merciful as your Heavenly Father is merciful. ... Be holy, for I, your God, am holy.*

If our response to God's invitation in the confessional is complete, forgiveness doesn't just make us feel better; it *recreates us.*

> Whoever is in Christ is a new creation: the old things have passed away; behold, new things have come.
>
> 2 Corinthians 5:17

Pope John Paul II, in one of his Holy Thursday addresses, demonstrates this by comparing our sacramental encounter with Christ in the confessional with the gospel story of Christ's surprise meeting with Zacchaeus (see Lk 19:1-10).

Jesus has entered Jericho and is moving through the city surrounded by a great crowd of people. Zacchaeus, the chief tax collector of Jericho, climbs a sycamore tree, presumably out of curiosity — perhaps comparable to the sometimes superficial way in which we approach the sacraments.

As Pope John Paul writes,

> Zacchaeus had no idea that the curiosity which had prompted him ... was already the fruit of a mercy which had preceded him, attracted him, and was about to change him in the depths of his heart.

Jesus, arriving at the tree, looks up at Zacchaeus and calls him by name, saying, "Zacchaeus, come down quickly, for today I must stay at your house" (Lk 19:5).

"The home of this sinner," Pope John Paul explains, "is about to become a place of revelation, the scene of a miracle of mercy." But, since mercy "reaches fulfilment to the extent that it meets a response" (#6), this miracle will not happen if Zacchaeus cannot free his heart from his former "unjust and fraudulent ways."

Penetrated by the gaze of Christ and stunned at hearing himself called by name in such a personal and friendly way, Zacchaeus responds to Christ immediately: "He came down quickly and received him with joy" (Lk 19:6).

His change of heart is complete; he promises to give half of his wealth to the poor and to repay four-fold all whom he has defrauded, and Jesus replies, "Today salvation has come to this house" (Lk 19:9).

And Pope John Paul points out:

> This is what happens in every sacramental encounter. We must not think that it is the sinner, through his own independent journey of conversion, who earns mercy. On the contrary, it is mercy that impels him along the path of conversion.

> Left to himself, man can do nothing and he deserves nothing. Before being man's journey to God, confession is God's arrival at a person's home.

How I wish I had understood this years ago! *Confession is God's arrival at my home.* He knows each of us, as He knew Zacchaeus. He sees everything — all our sins, all our weaknesses, even our most hidden thoughts — but He also sees the beautiful "not yet" that even we, ourselves, may not see, the "not yet" of who we are but have not yet become. And with His searing, healing, all-embracing gaze of love, He calls us by name and invites Himself into our home

We don't *go* to confession; we are *called* to this encounter with Jesus — the one whom we love because He has first loved us. Trusting in this love, we enter into this sacramental encounter, called by name to change our hearts and our lives, and become who we already are in the mind of God.

Having received the new wine in new skins, we can sing with St. Catherine of Siena,

> I have clothed myself with your likeness and have seen what I shall be. ... You are my creator, ... and I am your creature. You have made me a new creation in the blood of your son.

SECRET 7
You Have to Let Go of Your Chains!

*Let us throw off the chains
that prevent us from following Him.*

St. Augustine

The concepts that we've seen so far could all be summed up as the "good news" — the good news that the Father of Mercies is always loving us, always ready, not only to forgive, but also to heal and restore us as His children, recreating us in His image and likeness.

Now here's the "bad news." There are barriers —

often unknown and unintentional — that can block all this, block His love, His forgiveness, His healing and restoration.

Something can block God? Yes! God, because He is a completely free being, dared to create *us* as free beings, formed to be just *like* Him so that we could eventually live *with* Him forever.

Having thus chosen to create us free, God will never violate that freedom. He will relentlessly pursue us with His love to help us make right choices, but He will never force His love upon us, and there are things that we do that can block His love.

Barrier #1: Lack of Faith

Think back on the Gospels. There were some places (including His own hometown), where Christ could not perform miracles because of the people's lack of faith. (see Mk 6:4-5). And there are several contrasting instances where Christ specifically attributed His power to the degree of a person's faith: "Your faith has made you well" (see Mt 9:22; Mk 10:52; Lk 7:50; Lk 18:42).

The kind of faith that is needed is not just a belief, but a living faith put into action as trust: a reliance upon God, confident that He really does love you and is willing and able to "turn all things to good" in your life. Trust draws His mercy: lack of trust blocks it.

He revealed this in many ways to St Faustina, even to the extent of telling her:

> **I am making Myself dependent upon your trust: if your trust is great, then My generosity will be without limit.**
>
> *Diary* 548

Barrier #2: Idolatry

"Now, wait a minute. I don't worship idols!"

Oh, yes, you do. No, you probably haven't made a golden calf and set it up on a little altar in your house, bowing down before it as if it were a living being with divine power. But, as the *Catechism* explains, there's a lot more to idolatry than this.

> Idolatry not only refers to false pagan worship. … Idolatry consists in divinizing what is not God.
>
> #2113

Divinizing what is not God — clearly forbidden in the first of the ten commandments: "I am the Lord your God. … You shall have no other gods before me" (Ex 20:2-3 NRSV). … "Worship the Lord your God, … him alone shall you serve" (Lk 4:8).

What are these "other gods" that we are told not to serve? The *Catechism* makes it clear that *anything* can become an idol if we allow it to take God's rightful place as Lord (see #2114).

As Scott Hahn explains, "All sin is, in some sense, a form of idolatry: to prefer the creature to the creator, the gift to the giver."

It can even be something good — your job, your appearance, your social life, sporting events, even religious activities — anything you've become so attached to that you are neglecting your responsibilities to other people and failing to keep God at the center of your life.

Who's on the Throne?

Let me suggest an image that I've found really helpful in recognizing what our idols are. Remember the gospel passage where Christ tells us that the kingdom of God is within (see Lk 17:21)? Well your heart is the kingdom and, as in every kingdom, there's a king, seated on a throne.

So the question to ask is, "Who's on the throne?" If it's not Jesus Christ, you've got a problem. What's the solution? The lyrics of an old hymn express it really well: "Cast all false idols from the throne. The Lord is God and He alone."

Pope Francis points out that it's a question of priorities. He says that, whether we know it or not, we all have "a very clear order of priority concerning the things we consider important." He explains that we need to recognize Christ as the Lord and really worship Him alone.

> Worshipping the Lord means giving him the place that he must have. ... Worshipping is stripping ourselves of our idols, even the most hidden ones, and choosing the Lord as the centre, the highway of our lives.

Don't miss the point here. *Things* are not the problem. *People* are not the problem. Particular *goals and activities* are not the problem. The problem is in *our craving and grasping* for gratification through these things. It's when our desires become so disordered that we become overly focused, attached, and dependent on anything other than God.

What's the ultimate result of these disordered desires? Bondage.

As Iain Matthew explains in *The Impact of God*, our idols enslave us, leaving us "glued to ourselves" so that we become hostages to our own needs.

To free ourselves, we need to refocus on Christ, asking *Him* to give us the love, peace, joy, security, fulfillment that we've been seeking elsewhere.

Barrier #3: The Father Wound

As we've seen, God is not just our creator, but our Father. We were each chosen by Him, fathered into existence, and formed in His image and likeness so that someday we can be with Him forever.

Whether we are conscious of it or not, every cell in our bodies, every aspect of our being, *longs to belong* to this Father and to live in His love. As if in anticipation of this ultimate destiny in God's plan, we each have a built-in desire and need to be loved, appreciated, affirmed, respected, approved, and valued.

So, every time someone in our lives who should reflect this fathering love fails to do so, we are wounded, often deeply wounded.

It can be an actual father or some other father figure: a mother, a brother or sister, a teacher, a priest, a boss, a friend — anyone whom you needed to reflect God's tender, affirming love and who instead reflected anger, criticism, disapproval, ridicule, rejection, indifference, betrayal — or some other negative response that leaves you feeling unvalued and unloved.

A lot of people can't believe in a loving God because they've never experienced that type of love. It has been denied them by the very people who should have shown it to them.

Like our idols, this woundedness can cripple and enslave us, causing us to block off part of our minds and hearts to other people and to God, unconsciously setting up within ourselves the barrier that I feel is the most dangerous and impenetrable of all:

Barrier #4: Unforgiveness

The *Catechism* has a beautiful and very detailed section on the Lord's Prayer. It begins by celebrating the incredible reality of God's love for us — that we can actually "dare" to call God our Father because He has adopted us as His *children*. We belong to Him, and His fatherly love for us "has no bounds" (#2793).

Sounds pretty good, huh? God's love has no bounds. The trouble is that our reception of it does. His love is unconditional, but our ability to receive it depends completely on one, all-important condition:

> And forgive us our trespasses *as we forgive* those who trespass against us.

The *Catechism* begins its explanation of this "strict requirement" by pointing out that, when we first start praying the Lord's prayer, we can pray with "bold confidence" because, though we are sinners, we feel a "firm hope in God's mercy, His forgiving love poured out for us through the sacraments" (#2839).

But the next paragraph clobbers us!

Now — and this is daunting —

Whoa! Time for a little grammar lesson. Notice those long dashes? They're called "em dashes." A writer uses this type of dash to interrupt a thought in order to emphasize something important.

The *Catechism* starts to tell us something and then interrupts itself to emphasize that what it's about to say is "daunting."

What does "daunting" mean? It means scary, frightening, worrisome. It's as if the *Catechism* is warning us of what's coming next and asking us:

> *Are you sitting down? Brace yourselves, because this is frightening!*

Then it continues:

> This outpouring of mercy cannot penetrate our hearts as long as we have not forgiven those who have trespassed against us.
>
> #2840

God is "our Father," and all He wants to do is

bless His children, pouring His love into our hearts. But this outpouring of God's love *"cannot penetrate"* our hearts if we have not forgiven those who have trespassed against us!

That *is* scary. That's real scary. And there's more:

> In refusing to forgive our brothers and sisters, our hearts are closed and their hardness makes them impervious to the Father's merciful love.
>
> #2840

Impervious. Do you know what that means? It means that *nothing* can get through. It's like water flowing over rock.

When I first read that, it scared me to death. I was going to daily Mass, receiving Communion, trying to say the Divine Mercy Chaplet every day, trying to say the Rosary, trying to be a good person. I've been a cradle Catholic all my life, and now the *Catechism* is telling me:

> *Big deal! Yeah, you're doing some things right, but there's a big problem. God's love can't get in, Vinny, because you have unforgiveness in your heart!*

Ouch! No wonder I keep going back to confession with the same stuff!. No wonder I keep having trouble making the changes I want to make in my life!

Back to the image we saw earlier: "Who's on the throne? Is Christ seated on the throne in my heart? Or has unforgiveness pushed Him off? Is Christ the ruler of my heart, or have anger, bitterness, and resentment hardened my heart and closed it to Him?

So I immediately sat down and tried to take an inventory of my heart. OK, who do I need to forgive? Who am I angry with? Who do I resent? Am I holding any grudges? Any unpleasant, hurtful memories still alive and kicking inside me, so that my relationship with another person has grown cold or hostile?

As people came to mind, I did my best to forgive them, and to offer them to God for forgiveness and blessing. It was freeing, and it felt good.

But I wasn't done. Having finally taken a good look at what was in my heart, I found that there was a lot of negative stuff that didn't really involve people — feelings of irritation, anger, frustration, resentment — not at people but at situations, circumstances, unfulfilled needs, unanswered prayers, derailed plans. I discovered that I needed to forgive life itself, with all its twists and turns. And, most of all, I found that I needed to forgive God for not following my scripts.

What I had suddenly realized is that, without knowing or intending it, I had reversed the Lord's Prayer. My heart wasn't reflecting what my lips were praying. Instead of accepting His will, moment-by-moment, I was trying to get Him to do my will. "Thy will be done" had become "My will be done," and since that wasn't happening, I was filled with all kinds of unforgiveness.

I mentioned that this happened without my knowing or intending it. That's a really important thing to remember. The different forms of unforgivenes, like all the other barriers we've seen, are not usually intentional.

We don't normally make a conscious decision to remain weak in our faith and trust, to make other things more important than God, to allow our woundedness to cripple us, or to fill our hearts with unforgiveness. Unless we learn to look for these barriers, we don't even know they're there. That's what makes them so dangerous and so paralyzing to us in our spiritual growth.

And speaking of paralyzing, there's another image I want to give you — the image of chains. (I'll bet you thought I'd never get to the title of this chapter. Honestly, I was starting to wonder myself. But here we are at last.)

Our sins are chains. Our doubts, worries, and anxieties are chains. Our idols are chains. Our wounds are chains, our feeings of unforgiveness are chains. They come in all different lengths and weights, but they're all chains, and they weigh us down.

St. Paul talks about the spiritual life as "running the race" (2 Tim 4:7). Well, I can't run a good race if I've got chains hanging around my neck. Sometimes I'm carrying so many chains that I can barely walk.

Several years ago, at a men's retreat, I presented this image in a very visual way (and it was a lot of fun). I began my talk by dragging in a huge bag of steel chains of varying thickness, length, and weight.

Earlier I had asked one of the men to help me. He was young and obviously very strong and athletic, worked out regularly at a fitness center, and had competed in various rock climbing and triathlon activities. I called him up to stand beside me and asked the men a ridiculous question: "If Jim and I were to run a race right now, who do you think would win?"

The laughter went on for quite a while.

I pulled a long, heavy chain out of my bag. "Do you know what this is? It's original sin." And I draped it over Jim's neck.

"Did you ever consciously do something you knew was wrong?" All the hands slowly went up, and I placed an assortment of smaller chains around his neck, identifying them as "deliberate sins."

There followed a whole series of questions: "Ever allowed anyone or anything to take up too much space in your mind and heart — success, money, career, hobby, etc.?" … "Ever had trouble freeing yourself from addictions or bad habits?" … "Ever felt criticized, misunderstood, abandoned, neglected, or abused by a father, a mother, an authority figure, an employer, a friend?"

With each new question, more and more chains were piled on poor Jim's neck.

Then the final set of questions: "Right now are

you holding a grudge against anyone?" ... "Is there anything you have trouble forgiving — a person who hurt you, an unpleasant situation, or even God, Himself?" ... "Any recurring feelings of anger, bitterness, or resentment you just can't let go of?" And I placed the largest, heaviest chain of all around Jim's neck: *"Unforgiveness."*

I turned to the men and asked, "If we were to race now, who do you think would win?"

What happened then was totally unrehearsed. Jim dropped to the floor on his knees and threw his arms to his side in the shape of a cross.

I thought at first that he had done it on purpose to add a bit of drama, but he assured me afterwards that he didn't. His knees had just suddenly given out under the weight of the chains, and he had thrown his arms out to keep his balance.

It was a perfect lead-in to what I wanted to say to the men: "The way we get rid of our chains is by giving them to Christ on the cross."

> It is Christ who redeemed us. ... He bore our burden in public view, fixed it to the cross, ... released our shackles, and

destroyed our chains. ... We are freed of these chains and liberated by the blood of Christ.

In Secret 5, I explained the Eternal Now and shared the first verse of a song I wrote that expressed how Christ reached out from the cross to heal us, taking all our sins into Himself and destroying them through His death, "once for all." But I also explained that we have to *access* this forgiveness and healing; we have to *do* something.

Back to Jim, kneeling on the floor in the form of a cross. I helped him to his feet and then reached my hands out to him:

Give them to me.

This part *had* been rehearsed. Jim hesitated, and then shook his head, backing away as if afraid, clinging to his chains. I reached out again and repeated,

Give them to me and be free of them.

He hesitated again, and then slowly removed one of the chains and placed it in my hands; then, one by one (more quickly now), all the others. I placed each one around my neck. Turning back to the men, I said to them — as I say to you now —

> *Christ, in the confessional, in the Eternal Now of the cross, is reaching out across time and space to take your chains. He is asking you to stop clinging to them and let them go so that he can destroy them and set you free.*

And with that, I took all the chains from around my neck and threw them on the floor.

The chains I'm talking about are not just the chains of the sinful behaviors we've already confessed. We've gotten rid of those. Any time I acknowledge my sin and give it to God, especially in the confessional, I'm giving it to Jesus Christ on the cross 2,000 years ago, and He's taking it. So we've lightened our load a bit that way.

What I want to get at is the chains that you and I have either not recognized or have not yet been able to give to Christ. He wants them. He wants to take them away. The Father wants us to be chainless. He wants us to be free. He created us as His children, but we're not free to *be* His children. Like Jim, we're too weighed down by these chains, especially the chains of unforgiveness forged by our wounds.

During my talks about confession, I often ask a set of questions similar to the ones I asked at the men's retreat: "Has anyone here ever felt really hurt by someone else — betrayed ... overlooked ... snubbed ... forgotten ... manipulated ... taken advantage of ... used ... mistreated in some way? Who here has ever had any kind of emotional, mental, physical violence done to them by somebody else?"

Then I ask them to look around the room. Every hand is always up.

Let's face it, we are all often hurt by people who don't treat us the way we should be treated, people who just aren't there when we need them to be, people who are inconsiderate, demanding, unreasonable, undependable, arrogant, critical, dishonest, and even downright nasty.

And sometimes life seems to kick us in the teeth through events, situations, and circumstances that we can't control and that often leave us disappointed, frustrated, angry, and depressed.

We all have these wounds! But the wounds aren't what cripple us and chain us to ourselves; it's the way we *respond* to them that does that.

The way we often tend to react when we've been hurt can cause a type of sin that kind of sneaks up on us so that we don't even know it's sin. Whenever we feel hurt in any way — victimized by other people, by situations, by life itself — there's a natural, human reaction to blame someone, to strike back somehow. So we respond with anger, resentment, bitterness, judgment, rebellion, and a whole bunch of other not so pleasant thoughts and feelings.

At times, our responses are very verbal, and we sin with our tongues. At other times, we don't say anything out loud; we just lock up all those negative reactions inside our hearts and minds where they continue to grow and eat away at us like cancerous sores.

Sometimes, we "say" things inside ourselves, things like, "I hate him!" ... "I don't ever want to be like her!" ... "What a jerk!" ... "I wish he were dead!" And on and on — you get the idea.

Every time you allow these kinds of things to

remain in your mind and heart, you place another chain around your neck. These are all forms of unforgiveness, and we need to get rid of them. As St.Paul writes,

> Put away from you all bitterness and wrath and anger and wrangling and slander, together with all malice, and be kind to one another, … forgiving one another, as God in Christ has forgiven you.
>
> Ephesians 4:31-32 NRSV

One of the things that makes it hard to get rid of this stuff is that our reactions often seem justifiable because we're "in the right." We have been wrongly treated by someone else, and we often take a kind of comfort in our hurt by "telling our stories," the stories of how we were victimized, how we were wronged.

Sometimes we just tell them in our own minds, "nursing and rehearsing." We go back over and over again the wounds we've had, and we dwell on them. And sometimes we tell our stories to others. The more we do this, the more it feeds our resentment and bitterness, and our rebellion against the person, the situation, and even God Himself.

It also becomes a habit. We become attached to telling our stories; it makes us feel righteous and imposed upon. And it helps us draw sympathy from others and justify ourselves for our negative responses: "Look at how I've been wronged. I have a right to feel the way I do!"

But it's not about being right. It's about choosing whether to bless or to curse.

At every intersection of our daily lives, you and I are presented with a choice. In this situation, this circumstance, this encounter with another person, am I going to respond with a blessing or a curse? Am I going to be a light in the darkness, or am I going to curse the darkness and thus become part of it?

St. Paul exhorts us:

> Bless those who persecute you. Bless and do not curse.
>
> Romans 12:14

And St. Peter adds:

> Do not repay evil for evil or abuse for abuse; but, on the contrary, repay with a

blessing. It is for this that you were called —
that you might inherit a blessing.

1 Peter 3:9 NRSV

How do I learn to bless when I feel like cursing —
when I feel I have a right to curse? By using a very
simple exercise called "The Three R's."

What are "The Three R's?" (I'm glad you asked.)

The Three R's

You're driving down the road, when suddenly someone cuts you off, and you have to
slam on your brakes. You growl inside, your
body tenses up, and your face turns into a
nasty snarl:

"What a jerk! Why don't you learn how
to drive?" Gradually you start to relax, and
then you realize that you just chose to curse
instead of to bless. What do you do? Use
the Three R's:

1. Repent. "Oh, Lord, there I go again.
I'm sorry, Lord. I repent of that reaction; I
repent of the thoughts, the judgments, the
anger, the words I uttered."

2. Revoke. "I revoke all those negative, unkind thoughts, Lord. I un-think them, and I un-say those words."

3. Replace. "I replace those 'curses' with a blessing, Lord. I forgive him, and I bless him, and I ask that You bless him, Lord."

You can use the Three R's anytime, anyplace. Every time you become aware of any negative stuff inside you, just repent, revoke, and replace it. The more you get used to doing this, the more you will discover how often unforgiveness can sneak into your heart. I now use this prayer almost daily, sometimes several times a day. And it's so freeing!

Another way to learn to respond to people and situations with a blessing is to model yourself on Jesus.

"Jesus, on the night He was betrayed"...

Ever hear those words before? How did Jesus react to being wronged?

On the night He was betrayed, Jesus sat

around with his disciples complaining about the Pharisees and Saducees and all the mistreatment He had been receiving.

Or, how about this?

> On the night he was betrayed, Jesus walked off by Himself, reflecting on his misery, feeling sorry for Himself because nobody understood Him.

Or this?

> On the night He was betrayed, Jesus walked over to Judas and smacked him real hard.

Not very true to the scriptures, is it? What was Christ's reaction to betrayal? To violence? Even the awful violence on the cross?

Did He want to retaliate, to "get even?" Did He just tell His story to anyone who would listen? Did He go over and over it in His mind, nursing and rehearsing all the reasons why he was justified in feeling anger, bitterness, rebellion, judgment, and other forms of unforgiveness?

Christ was *right!* He hadn't done anything wrong; and yet He had been terribly violated as a person.

It's not a question of whether you are right or not!

You and I have been wronged by other people and maybe kicked around by life, too. That's real! But wallowing in our woundedness and binding ourselves with unforgiveness is not going to help.

How did Christ react? He said, "Father, forgive them because they don't know what they are doing." Father, forgive them. And Jesus Christ is saying to you — right now and at every moment of hurt — "Forgive, forgive, forgive."

Are there people you need to forgive? If so, you need to talk to them, in person if possible. If that's not possible, then you need to talk to them in your mind. Don't deny the pain; don't deny how wronged you feel. Just identify the hurt and forgive it:

"Dad, you mistreated me terribly, and it was wrong. It was awful. You shouldn't have done it, and it hurt me, but I forgive you; and I ask God to forgive you; and I bless you."

Anytime you do that, you've just unchained yourself. If you've ever said, "I don't ever want to be like my mom," or anything similar, unsay it. Use the Three R's:

> *"Lord, I repent of that; and I repent of the anger and bitterness and judgment I feel now in my heart. I revoke it Lord; I unsay it. And I replace it Lord. I bless her, and I ask you to bless her."*

I remember a young man who came up after one of my talks on unforgiveness. He told me that he had suddenly remembered that, at one point, as a boy, he had wished his father dead. So he took a minute to talk to God about it and unwish it:

> *"Lord, I unwish that. I unsay the thought that was in my mind. I want him alive. I forgive him."*

He immediately felt something lift off him, a burden he hadn't even known he was carrying all those years.

In a similar way, at a retreat we were giving, a woman came up to us, obviously very distraught, and asked us to pray with her. She told us that a memory had just surfaced, a memory so deeply buried that she hadn't known it was there.

For the first time in over forty years she was suddenly face-to-face with the reality that her father had sexually abused her when she was a child.

We led her through a prayer of forgiveness and blessing and, when she was finally able to face the hurt, let go of it, and express forgiveness, the change that came over her was amazing to see. She was a different person. After all those years, she was free.

Other people have voiced a different problem. They've done their best to forgive, but the memories keep coming back, the hurt resurfaces, and the negative feelings start to take hold again:

"I can forgive, but I can't forget."

A pretty common experience. So, what do you do about it? Some people will tell you, "Well, you just need to keep trying, you know, work harder at it, because you need to forgive *and* forget."

That may sound like sage advice, but it's totally wrong — and it's not helpful. Suggesting that there's something wrong with people because they can't forget an injury simply causes more pain, more shame, and more inability to forgive it completely and be free of its crippling power.

This is a really important point, so if you're falling asleep while you're reading this, wake up for a minute and really hear this: *Yes, you need to forgive; but you will not be able to forget.* The next time you hear someone say "Forgive and forget," just tell them to go read the *Catechism.*

As we've seen, the *Catechism* strongly emphasizes the necessity of forgiveness, but it also acknowledges the reality that we don't have the power "not to feel" an offense. We don't have the power "to forget an offense" (#2843).

Most of us have experienced this. We honestly and sincerely try to forgive, but then something happens that reminds us of the event, and as the memory leaps unbidden into our minds, we relive it; we feel the hurt again and, if we try to deny the pain or make it go away, we only increase its negative power and fall back into unforgiveness.

What can we do? The *Catechism* tells us:

> It is not in our power not to feel or to forget an offense. But the heart that offers itself to the Holy Spirit turns injury into compassion and purifies the memory in transforming the hurt into intercession.
>
> #2843

What does that mean? It means don't try to forget. Don't deny the memory. Let it come. And don't deny the hurt that comes with it. Accept it and *use* it.

How? Just ask for the grace to truly forgive the person who hurt you, and then every time the old tapes start playing in your mind and you feel the hurt again, offer it to the Holy Spirit as a prayer *for that person*. As you do this, gradually your memory is purified, your heart is healed, and the hurt loses its power over you. You thus become able to fulfill Christ's command to "love your enemies and pray for those who persecute you" (Mt 5:44).

(If the hurt is too deep, and you can't do this right away, don't beat yourself up about it. Be patient with yourself, and offer your heart to the Holy Spirit. Your heart has been hurt and needs to be healed, and healing takes time.)

As I write this, I have an image in my mind of people in chains — people reading this book — people who have been wounded by a father or a father figure, people whose children have died, people who've been raped, people whose spouses have left, people who have been victimized in so many ways, people whose woundedness has left them trapped by sin and paralyzed by guilt and shame.

Some are clinging to their chains, holding on to their pain, keeping it alive by telling their stories over and over. Others are trying to escape their pain by burying their wounds deep inside to protect themselves from the memories that might re-open them.

And over them all, I see Christ on the cross, reaching out with such tenderness, wanting to break their chains and set them free.

I just want to encourage you: don't hold on to your pain. Don't cling to it and don't run from it. Don't keep telling your story (to yourself or anyone else), and don't try to bury the memories, but dare to give it all to God. "OK, Lord, help me to see what's in my heart. Are there wounds there that have never healed? Is there any anger, bitterness, resentment, unforgiveness there? What am I holding onto Lord? What are the chains that I need to let go of and give to you?"

> Some lay in darkness and in gloom, prisoners in misery and chains. Then they cried to the Lord in their need, and He rescued them from their distress. He led them forth from darkness and gloom and broke their chains to pieces.
>
> Psalm 107:10,13

We need to cry out to the Lord and let Him break our chains to pieces. And there's no better place to do this than the confessional.

To whatever extent you have unforgiveness in your heart, get rid of it. Identify it, name it, talk to God about it. As soon as you can, get into the confessional about it, whether you see any sin connected to it or not.

As we've seen, the confessional is a place for healing wounds. It is not just a place to go with your sins. Confession is an ongoing process of healing.

Earlier I shared the first verse of a song I wrote about Christ seeing us from the cross and reaching out to take our sins. The second verse expresses a prayer that I invite you to pray with me as, from *our* crosses, our places of pain, we look out and see Him, let go of the chains that bind us, and allow Him to heal us:

From my cross,
I see Your face and love You.
I feel Your touch
and trust that You can heal me.
Into Your hands
I place the chains my sins have made,
and I say, "Yes, my God,
restore me in Your love."

YOU HAVE TO LET GO OF YOUR CHAINS

AFTERWORD
Change Your Oil!

It would be illusory to desire to reach holiness ...
without partaking frequently of this
sacrament of conversion and sanctification.

Pope John Paul II

I hope you didn't stop reading after Secret 7. I know it was a pretty long chapter (sorry about that), but it wasn't the end. I still have something pretty important to tell you.

Here in the Afterword, I want to revisit something I shared in the Foreword — because I want to convince you of something:

Don't just "go" to confession; go a lot!

If you forget most of what I've told you here, at least remember that confession is not just about forgiveness of bad behavior, not a one-time fix, but a process of healing and education that helps us grow.

If it were just a one-time fix, that would mean that I only have to go when something in me is seriously "broken." But since it's a process, that means I'm getting something in "installments," bit by bit, step by step, confession by confession. It means that the more you go, the more you *grow*.

> *So, please, go often — and don't go just thinking about sin! Go with the consciousness of the things that we've seen here: Go for grace! Go to grow!*

I mentioned earlier that what we tend to do when we go to confession is confess our *sins* — but not the *roots* of our sins. So our sins are forgiven, but what caused us to sin has not been healed. We think that the sin is the problem. But it's not. The problem is what's been building up in us in terms of our attitudes, our habits, our sinful*ness*, our weakness, our human condition, our failure to *grow* in our relationship with God.

We need to look deeper, asking the Holy Spirit, "Come in. Probe my heart. Reveal to me what the real problems are. What are the things that are leading me into sin? What disordered desires or attitudes have I embraced? Where do I need mercy most? Where do I need healing? Where do I need to grow?"

When you really understand and value this sacrament, each time you go brings one more installment of holiness, one more degree of tranformation, one more infusion of Christ into your heart so that you can become that new wine skin, that new creation, restored in His image and likeness, so that you can ultimately be with Him forever.

So don't just go when you "need to" because you've fallen into serious sin. Go often for the grace that will help you *avoid* sin!

Pope Benedict XVI explains that it's important and necessary to be aware of our sins and to sincerely accuse ourselves of them in confession. But if we focus only on sin, we may fail to experience the central reality of this sacrament.

What's the central reality?

> The personal encounter with God, the Father of goodness and mercy. It is not *sin* that is at the heart of the sacramental celebration, but rather *God's mercy*.

He makes it clear that when we go to confession frequently, not just for forgiveness, but "to experience the Heavenly Father's merciful love," it helps us reorient our lives toward continual conversion:

> We must always aspire to conversion. ... When we receive the sacrament of Reconciliation frequently, the desire for Gospel perfection is kept alive. ... If this constant desire is absent, the celebration of the sacrament unfortunately risks becoming something formal that has no effect on the fabric of daily life.

In his book *Living the Sacraments*, Fr. David Knight writes that, in order to allow confession to have a real effect on our daily lives, we need to use it "on a regular basis" as an "ongoing sacrament of growth," not simply as a turning away *from* sin, but as a turning *to* growing as disciples of Jesus:

> Confession used only for forgiveness is a conversion *from*. Confession used as a guide and incentive to spiritual growth is a conversion *to* a more insightful, radical, authentic following of Jesus Christ. ...

I think many of us tend to view confession the same way we view taking our car to the garage for a repair job. We think that confession is when we need a major overhaul. We're not running right, so we have to get "fixed." We should instead be thinking of confession as "maintenance."

Confession should be an oil change.

I remember when I got my first really nice car. It was only two years old, and it only had 12,000 miles on it. One of my friends said, "Let me tell you something. No matter what else you do, change the oil every 3,000 miles, and that car will keep running." It turned out to be really good advice.

If you've bought any major appliances lately, you were probably offered a "maintenance agreement." It costs you extra, but, with a maintenace agreement, when things go wrong, you can have them fixed. Sometimes the agreement covers parts only, and sometimes it's free parts and labor.

I like to think of confession as part of our maintenance agreement with Christ. We each come with a lifetime warranty. And if anything ever goes wrong, Christ will replace everything free. Parts and labor. Everything's free. Forever. That's our maintenance agreement. And it doesn't cost us a nickel more. All we have to do is take advantage of that. We come to confession as a part of that maintenance agreement.

If you buy a new car, the maintenance agreement on it is something like 50,000 miles or 5 years, whichever comes first. But this agreement only deals with factory defects or things that go wrong in the normal course of events. If you abuse the product, you've ruined the warranty.

God even lets us abuse the product. He still fulfills the lifetime warranty. But, in a practical sense, what is necessary is the same thing we find in an automobile agreement: there are certain required times for regular maintenance.

A manufacturer knows that if you don't ensure regular maintenance for the product, it's going to break — and then the company will have to fix it to honor its warranty. So you have to adhere to a regular schedule of preventative maintenance.

Just from checking the oil, you can see that, over a period of time, even if the car is running fine, impurities slip in. They mix with the oil, and the oil gets heavy and thick and dark, and it just doesn't do the job as well. So eventually, the car doesn't run as well, and it wears out faster.

But, if you put fresh oil in every 3,000 miles and replace the oil filter, you remove the impurities before they create serious problems.

Let's compare this concept with confession. Let's say we have no "mortal" impurities. We are still "running" fine; nothing is "broken" — but the little impurities are steadily building up, and we are gradually wearing ourselves out.

Just as with a scheduled oil change, we should go

to confession "every 3,000 miles" — that is, regularly!

What do I mean by "regularly?" Well, let me start by giving you an example. I remember how surprised I was when I first heard that Pope John Paul II was in the habit of going to confession once a week. I was (and am) in awe of that man's holiness. And I thought to myself, "He goes to confession once a week? Why?"

Because he put a lot of miles on! Even literally. So he went to confession regularly to keep the "oil" of his life pure — to get a fresh injection of the "new life" of grace.

I find myself smiling as I write this, because it brings back the memory of a little conversation that often took place between me and my spritual director, Fr. George Kosicki.

At that time, we were working together on a daily basis at the National Shrine of The Divine Mercy. He had been my spiritual director, mentor, and friend for a long time, and he knew me probably better than I knew myself.

I had shared with him this image of confession as an oil change, not a motor job and, after that, every once and awhile, he would stop what he was doing and look at me with a little smile on his face:

> *You're looking a little "run down," Vinny.*
> *Is it time for an oil change?"*

I never had to ask him to hear my confession. He'd tell *me* when I needed to go! And he was always right. His question would make me stop and take a look at myself; and I'd realize that I was starting to get a little "dusty," a little "grimy and gritty." I wasn't conscious of any serious sin, but things just didn't seem quite right.

(My guess is that there are people in your life who could tell you when it's time for a little "maintenance," too.)

I've learned that, if I don't take advantage of that period of time when I haven't commited any serious sin, but I'm just aware of the fact that "the oil needs changing" — that's when sin is going to come in, and then I'm going to need a repair job. I need to make time for "regular maintenance," so that I don't reach the point where there's a big fall from grace.

I can imagine some of you reading this and shaking your heads:

> "Wait a minute! Are you telling me I should go to confession *before* I've done anything really wrong? That I should go even if I only have a few *venial* sins to confess? And that I should go *every week*?"

Well, on the weekly part of it, I could probably cut you some slack; maybe you could start by going every other week, or even once a month. The exact time table can vary from person to person.

The main thing is to get in the habit of going regularly, frequently, and with the right attitude.

As for the part about going even with only venial sins to confess, let's just say that I strongly reccommend it. And I'm not alone.

Pope John Paul II who, as we've already seen, went to confession weekly, encouraged others to do the same; and he wrote to his priests and bishops that they should make use of the sacrament themselves "frequently and with good dispositions"; and that "great importance must continue to be given to teaching the faithful also to make use of the sacrament … *for venial sins alone.*"

Pope Benedict stongly echoed this in *the Sacrament of Charity*, writing that "bishops have the pastoral duty … of encouraging frequent confession among the faithful …" and that "all priests should dedicate themselves with generosity, commitment, and competency to administering the sacrament of Reconciliation."

The official *Rite of Penance* also addresses the benefits of frequent confession of venial sins:

> Those who through daily weakness fall into venial sins draw strength from a repeated celebration of penance to gain the full freedom of the children of God.
>
> #7

"Repeated celebration." I like that phrase. Ultimately, what is it that we are repeatedly celebrating through frequent confession? *Mercy!*

The *Catechism of the Catholic Church* tells us:

> Without being strictly necessary, confes-

sion of everyday faults [venial sins] is nevertheless strongly recommended by the Church.

Indeed, the regular confession of our venial sins helps us form our conscience, fight against evil tendencies, let ourselves be healed by Christ, and progress in the life of the Spirit.

By receiving more frequently through this sacrament the gift of the Father's mercy, we are spurred to be merciful as He is merciful.

#1458

There's no better reason to go to confession, and to go often, than this: *to receive the Father's mercy and learn to be merciful ourselves.*

Pope Francis, in his homily on Divine Mercy Sunday in 2013, talks about this so beautifully! And he tells us something we all need to hear when we struggle with our failings — especially when we get discouraged and impatient with ourselves. He talks about the patience and tenderness of God who, unlike us, doesn't need everything all at once:

God is patient with us because he loves

us, and those who love are able to understand, to hope, to inspire confidence; they do not give up, they do not burn bridges, they are able to forgive. Let us remember this . . . . God always waits for us, even when we have left him behind! He is never far from us, and if we return to him, he is ready to embrace us.

Reflecting on the prodigal son story — which he calls "the parable of the merciful Father — he reminds us that the Father had "never forgotten his son," but was waiting for him "every hour of every day." In spite of all that he had done, the son was "always in his Father's heart."

The Father had "never for a second stopped thinking about him," and when the son returns, he receives "the tenderness of God without reproach."

Wow! This is real! This is confession! No mattter where you are in your life, no matter what you have done or not done, no matter what your failings, weaknesses, sins, the Father has not forgotten you. You are always in His heart. He never stops thinking about you. He is always waiting for you and, when you return to Him, He will embrace you with divine tenderness, without reproach.

The Holy Father continues:

> Maybe someone among us here is thinking: my sin is so great, I am as far from God as the younger son in the parable. … I don't have the courage to go back, to believe that God can welcome me and that he is waiting for me. …
>
> But God is indeed waiting for you; he asks of you only the courage to go to him. … Don't be afraid, go to him, he is waiting for you, he will take care of everything.

The pope ends his homily with what, to me, seems like a perfect way for me to end this book, inviting you to enter into a new journey to joy in the confessional, a new, transforming pathway into healing and holiness:

> Let us be enveloped by the mercy of God; let us trust in his patience, which always gives us more time. Let us find the courage to return to his house, to dwell in his loving wounds, allowing ourselves be

loved by him and to encounter his mercy. We will feel his wonderful tenderness, we will feel his embrace, and we too will become more capable of mercy, patience, forgiveness and love.

$\mathscr{B}$ONUS SECRET
Don't Forget the Hors D'oeuvres

The reception of this sacrament ought to be
prepared for by an examination of conscience.

Catechism #1454

O kay, I'll be honest. I'm the one who forgot. there's something I wanted to share with you that has really helped me, but I've already used up all my 7 secrets. So, you get a "bonus" secret — and this one may actually be the "secret" that is most deeply hidden, the one most often forgotten.

And somehow it seems right to me to end with the beginning. *Before* you go to confession there are some things you should do in preparation. So, here we go. I want to offer you some "hor d'oeuvres" — some spiritual antipasti to get you ready for the main meal.

For much of my life, I didn't really know that my experience in the confessional would be much better if I prepared for it. I would usually just go. At best, I would take a few minutes to think about what I was going to say, but no real preparation.

So I want to give you a few sample examens, a list of Ten "Commandments" of Confession, some Confession Psalms, and a few links to other resources you may find helpful for prayerful preparation. Mostly, these will be little reminders of the things already discussed in the book, but there are two points I want to especially emphasize about preparing for confession.

Point # 1: Give it to Mary

She is the Mother of Divine Mercy, the one who understands mercy most, the one given to us as our Mother by Christ from the cross. Ask her to help you make a good confession, to intercede for you for the guidance of the Holy Spirit, and to accompany with you into the confessional. As Pope Francis explains, "She is our Mother, who always comes in haste when we need help," just as she went in haste to help her cousin Elizabeth.

Point #2. Pray for Your Confessor

Yes, pray for your confessor — and realize that part of his "job" is to pray for you.

What? The priest is supposed to pray for me? Yes. I never knew that, and I've had several priests tell me that they never knew it either. It wasn't taught to them in the seminary. But here's what the *Catechism* says about the duties of the priest:

> He must ... lead the penitent with patience toward healing and full maturity. He must pray and do penance for his penitent, entrusting him to the Lord's mercy.
>
> #1466

When I go to confession, my confessor and I just

sit there and pray together for a few minutes before we do anything else. What a difference it makes!

Okay, so my confessor should pray for me. But why should I pray for him? Because he's a person, too! Yes, he's consecrated his life to God and has been set apart to act *in persona Christi,* but he's still human (and usually over-worked and under-appreciated). Your prayer will help him — and it will help you.

St. Faustina writes:

> I came to understand one thing: that I must pray much for each of my confessors, that he might obtain the light of the Holy Spirit, for when I approach the confessional without first praying fervently, the confessor does not understand me very well.
>
> *Diary,* 647

So, do yourself and your confessor a big favor, and take some time to pray for him before you go into the confessional.

Okay, now you can take a look at the Examen and the other 'hors d'ouevres I've prepared for you. May they "whet your appetite" and help you to experience confession as a feast of grace.

7-Step Examen

1. What things keep showing up on my "list" in the confessional? (What habits, behaviors, vices, addictions do I seem to have most trouble changing?)

2. What are the root problems that are making it hard for me to make progress in these areas?

3. What areas of my life have I not yet submitted to the Lordship of Christ? Where am I not at peace?

4. What wounds do I have that need healing? Where am I hurting?

5. What person, situation, or event am I still resentful, bitter, or angry about? Who do I need to forgive (God, myself, others)?

6. Confession calls for a "radical reorientation" of my entire life. In what way(s) am I most unlike Jesus? What do I need to change?

7. What one thing can I resolve to change right now, trusting in God's grace?

Love is Patient Examen
(See how you measure up)

I am patient; I am kind; I am not envious or boastful or arrogant or rude. I do not insist on my own way; I am not irritable or resentful; I do not rejoice in wrongdoing, but rejoice in the truth. I bear all things, believe all things, hope all things, endure all things.

Based on 1 Corinthians 13:4-7

Other Examens:

There are many other examinations of conscience available, mostly based on the Ten Commandments or the Beatitudes. One excellent and comprehensive examen is from the *Handbook of Prayers*, edited by Fr. James Socias. It can also be found in the back of Scott Hahn's book, *Lord, Have Mercy: The Healing Power of Confession.* (Both books available on amazon.com)

Here are some links to some online examens (or you can do a search for many others):

usccb.org/prayer-and-worship/sacraments/penance/examinations-of-conscience.cfm

kofc.org/en/resources/cis/devotion

lifeteen.com/examination-of-conscience-pdf

catholicscomehome.org/what-is-the-sacrament-of-confession

ewtn.com/library/spirit/examcons.txt

Ten "Commandments" of Confession

1. Go frequently, even just for venial sins.

2. Take the time to prepare with prayer.

3. Turn to Mary, Mother of Mercy, to pray for you.

4. Call upon the Holy Spirit to convict you of your sins (show you your sins and your sinfulness).

5. Meditate upon the Passion of Christ to stir up the "Tears of Repentance."

6. Discern the areas where you are in most need of God's mercy.

7. Pray for your confessor. He is instructed by the Church to pray for you, so you, in turn should pray for the light of the Holy Spirit to guide him.

8. Don't just focus on behaviors. Focus on the root problems, sinful attitudes, miseries, and wounds of your heart.

9. Give thanks for your healing.

10. Do penance.

Confession Psalms
for Prayerful Reflection

Psalm 51
O God, Have Mercy on Me

Have mercy on me, God, in your kindness.
In your compassion blot out my offense.
O wash me more and more from my guilt
and cleanse me from my sin.

My offenses truly I know them;
my sin is always before me
Against you, you alone, have I sinned;
what is evil in your sight I have done. ...

Indeed you love truth in the heart:
Then in the secret of my heart teach me wisdom.
O purify me, then I shall be clean;
O wash me, I shall be whiter than snow. ...

Make me hear rejoicing and gladness,
that the bones you have crushed may revive.
From my sins turn away your face
and blot out all my guilt.

A pure heart create for me, O God,
put a steadfast spirit within me.
Do not cast me away from your presence,
nor deprive me of your holy spirit.

Give me again the joy of your help;
with a spirit of fervor sustain me,
that I may teach transgressors your ways
and sinners may return to you.

O rescue me, God, my helper,
and my tongue shall ring out your goodness.
O Lord, open my lips
and my mouth shall decare your praise

For in sacrifice you take no delight,
burnt offering from me you would refuse,
my sacrifice, a contrite spirit.
A humbled, contrite heart you will not spurn.

Excerpted from *The Liturgy of the Hours*, Vol. 3
(New York: Catholic Book Publishing, 1976), p.
790.

Psalm 103
(Personalized Excerpts)

I give thanks to You, O Lord, with all my being.
I give thanks to You and will never forget
all Your blessings.
You forgive all my sins; You heal all my ills;
You redeem my life from the grave;
You crown me with love and compassion;
You fill my life with good things,
renewing my youth.

Lord, You are compassion and love,
slow to anger and rich in mercy.
You do not treat us according to our sins,
nor repay us according to our faults.
As far as the east is from the west,
so far do You remove our sins.
As a father has compassion on his children,
so You have mercy on those who revere You.

See *The Liturgy of the Hours*, Vol. 3 (New York: Catholic Book Publishing, 1976), p. 1188.

Psalm 130
(Personalized Excerpts)

Out of the depths I cry to You, O Lord,
Lord, hear my voice!
O let Your ears be attentive
to the voice of my pleading.

If You, O Lord, should mark our guilt,
Lord, who would survive?
But with You is found forgiveness:
for this I revere You.

My soul is waiting for You, O Lord.
I count on Your word.
My soul is longing for You
more than watchman for daybreak.
(Let the watchman count on daybreak
and I on the Lord.)

Because with You, O Lord, there is mercy
and fullness of redemption.
You will redeem me
from all my iniquity.

See *The Liturgy of the Hours,* Vol. 3 (New York:
Catholic Book Publishing, 1976), p. 130.

Notes, Sources and References

FOREWORD
Beyond the Grocery List

Page 1: "With joy and trust …" Pope John Paul II, *Letter to Priests for Holy Thursday*, #4, March 17, 2002.

Page 5: "Let us ask Christ …" Pope John Paul II, *Letter to Priests for Holy Thursday*, #10, 11, March 25, 2001.

SECRET 1

Sin Doesn't Change God

Page 9: "We are not some casual and meaningless product …" Pope Benedict XVI, Installation Homily, April 24, 2005.

Page 10: "The essence of sin is our refusal of divine sonship." Scott Hahn, *A Father Who Keeps his Promises* (Ann Arbor, MI: Servent Publications, 1998), p. 20.

Page 16: "The son is up early …" St. John of the Cross, *Living Flame*, 46-7, as cited by Iain Matthew, *The Impact of God* (London: Hodder & Stoughton, 1995), p. 75.

Page 19: "God is seen by those who have the capacity to see him …" Theophilus of Antioch, from the book addressed to Autolycus, as cited in *The Liturgy of the Hours*, Vol. 2 (New York: Catholic Book Publishing, 1976), p. 240.

SECRET 2

It's Not Just about Forgiveness

Page 35: "a sacrament of enlightenment ... a precious light for the path of perfection ..." Pope John Paul II, Vatican City, March 27, 2004, at the internal forum of the Tribunal of the Apostolic Penitentiary.

Page 35: "called to take on the role of father, spiritual guide, teacher, and educator." Pope Benedict XVI, *Address of His Holiness Benedict XVI to the Confessers who Serve in the Four Papal Basilicas of Rome*, February 19, 2007

Page 38: "is permeated by an awareness of a deeper loss ..." Pope John Paul II, *Rich in Mercy*, #5.

Page 41: "To the blind man whom he healed, Jesus reveals that he has come into the world for judgment ..." Pope Benedict XVI, *Angelus* address, March 2, 2008.

SECRET 3

Your Sin is Different from My Sin

Page 47: "… distorted attitudes …" Fr. David Knight, *Living the Sacraments: A Call to Conversion* (Huntington IN: Our Sunday Visitor, 1984, p.28.

Page 63: "Every sin is simply a failure to respond as we should." Fr. David Knight, *An Armchair Retreat* (Huntington IN: Our Sunday Visitor, 1987), p.77.

SECRET 4

Confession is Never Really Private

Page 70: "By his ordination, the priest is granted sacred power …" Archbishop José Gomez, *The Tender Mercy of God: A Pastoral Letter to the People of God of San Antonio,* February 21, 2007, #5.

Page 70: "In the sacrament of Reconciliation we are all invited …" Pope John Paul II, Homily, Dublin, September 29, 1979, #6.

Page 71: "a more personal encounter ..." Pope John Paul II, Homily during Mass at The Phoenix Park, Dublin, September 29, 1979, #6, September 29, 1979, #6.

Page 71: "not to live confession as a rite, ..." Fr. Raniero Cantalamessa. Lenten Meditation to the Papal Household, April 2, 2004.

Page 79: "Reconciliation is principally a gift ..." Pope John Paul II, in his Apostolic Exhortation, *Reconciliation and Penance,* December2, 1984, # 5.

Page 79: ""to make their penitents experience the Heavenly Father's merciful love ..." Pope Benedict XVI, Address of March 7, 2008.

Page 80: "call to conversion is an encouragement to return to the arms of God ..." Pope Benedict XVI, General Audience, February 6, 2008.

Page 80: "Did not Christ say that our Father, ..." Pope John Paul II, *Rich in Mercy,* #2.

Page 81: "In going to confession we are like the prodigal son …" Archbishop José Gomez, *The Tender Mercy of God: A Pastoral Letter to the People of God of San Antonio*, February 21, 2007, #23.

Page 87: "When we sin, we 'disown' God as our Father …" Archbishop José Gomez, *The Tender Mercy of God: A Pastoral Letter to the People of God of San Antonio*, February 21, 2007, #12.

SECRET 5
You've Got Mail!

Page 92: "The Way of the Cross is not something of the past …" Pope Benedict XVI, Address after the Way of the Cross, Rome, April 15, 2006.

Page 95: "concentrated forever …" Pope John Paul II, *Ecclesia de Eucharistia*, #5.

Page 95: "applies to men and women today …" Pope John Paul II, *On the Eucharist in its Relationship to the Church*, #12.

Page 96: "should be considered alongside the importance of the Eucharist itself." Pope John Paul II, Closing Address, 1983 Synod of Bishops.

Page 104: "God created us without us ..." St. Augustine, *Sermo 169*, as cited in the *Catechism of the Catholic Church, # 1847*.

Page 106: "Why the Robin's Breast is Red." James Ryder Randall, *The Catholic Anthology* (New York: The Macmillan Co., 1947), p.284.

Page 113: "Ring out the old, ring in the new." Alfred Lord Tennyson, "Ring Out Wild Bells," from *In Memoriam*, 1849.

SECRET 6

New Wine Needs New Skins

Page 125: "*Go, and sin no more. ...*" Paraphrase of several scriptural passages. See Jn 8:11; Jn 14:34; Col 3:12-13; Lk 6:36; Lev 19:2.

Page 126: "Zacchaeus had no idea that ..." Pope John Paul II, *Letter to Priests for Holy Thursday*, March 21, 2002, #5.

Page 126: "The home of ..." Pope John Paul II, *Letter to Priests*, March 21, 2002, #6.

Page 127: "This is what happens ..." Pope John Paul II, *Letter to Priests*, March 21, 2002, #6.

Page 128: "I have clothed myself ..." St. Catherine of Siena, *On Divine Providence*, as cited in *The Liturgy of the Hours*, Vol. 2 (New York: Catholic Book Publishing, 1976), p. 1794.

SECRET 7

You have to Let Go of Your Chains

Page 131: "Let us throw off ..." St. Augustine, from A treatise on John, as cited in *The Liturgy of the Hours*, Vol. 2 (New York: Catholic Book Publishing, 1976), p. 276.

Page 134: "All sin is, in some sense ..." Scott Hahn, *Lord Have Mercy: The Healing Power of Confession* (New York, Doubleday, 2003), p. 123.

Page 135: "a very clear order of priority ..." Pope Francis, Homily, April 14, 2013.

Page 136: "glued ..." Iain Matthew, *The Impact of God* (London: Hodder & Stoughton, 1995), p. 47.

Page 136: "It is Christ who redeemed us ..." St. Pacian, as cited in *The Liturgy of the Hours,* Vol. 2 (New York: Catholic Book Publishing, 1976), p. 116.

Page 162: "Some lay in darkness and in gloom ..." Psalm 107, The Grail (England), 1963 and published by Collins, London, 1963.

AFTERWORD
Change Your Oil!

Page 165: "It woud be illusory ..." Pope John Paul II, Address in Rome, March 27, 2004.

Page 168: "The personal encounter with God" ..."
Pope Benedict XVI, Address of March 7, 2008.

Page 168: "We must always aspire to conversion ..." Pope Benedict XVI, Address of March 7, 2008.

Page 169: "Confession used only for forgiveness is a conversion from ..." Fr. David Knight, *Living the Sacraments: A Call to Conversion* (Huntington IN: Our Sunday Visitor, 1984, p.26.

Page 174: "Frequently and with good dispositions ..." Pope John Paul II, in his Apostolic Exhortation, *Reconciliation and Penance,* December 2, 1984, # 31:IV.

Page 174: "Great importance must continue to be given ..." Pope John Paul II, in his Apostolic Exhortation, *Reconciliation and Penance,* December 2, 1984, # 32.

Page 175: "Bishops have the pastoral duty ..." Pope Benedict XVI, *Sacrament of Charity*, #21.

Page 176: "God is patient with us because he loves us" … Pope Francis, Divine Mercy Sunday Homily, April 7, 2013, #2.

Page 177: "never forgotten his son … always in his Father's heart … the tenderness of God without reproach …" Pope Francis, Divine Mercy Sunday Homily, April 7, 2013, #2.

Page 178: "Maybe someone here is thinking …" Pope Francis, Divine Mercy Sunday Homily, April 7, 2013, #3.

Page 178: "Let us be enveloped …" Pope Francis, Divine Mercy Sunday Homily, April 7, 2013, #3.

BONUS SECRET
Don't Forget the Hors d'ouevres

Page 183: "She is our Mother …" Pope Francis, Homily, Parish of Prima Porta in Rome, May 26, 2013.

Flynn Family Music

Benedictus
Traditional Holy Hour hymns with new arrangements and an Irish touch. Perfect for Holy Hours, healing services, Adoration, or quiet prayer time. **$15.99**

Endless Mercy
Gentle, healing songs by Vinny Flynn to soothe your spirit or comfort a loved one. Often used for retreats, prayer meetings, and healing services. **$15.99**

Through the Darkness
Erin Flynn's haunting vocals on this award-winning album will touch the depths of your soul, inspiring you to deeper love and trust in God. **$15.99**

Cry Out
John Flynn's collection of original Catholic liturgical songs with a contemporary music style and lyrics that pull the listener into the heart of worship. **$15.99**

Beyond the Veil
Winner of 3 Unity Awards, including "2010 Praise & Worship Album of the Year," this CD by Brian Flynn' presents solid Catholic teaching in beautiful, original songs, featured on EWTN. **$16.99**

We Sing Your Praise II
A collection of inspirational songs from the Flynn family CDs. Includes selections from Benedictus, Cry Out, Endless Mercy, In the Sight of the Angels, and Through the Darkness. **$15.99**

**Order online at www.mercysong.com
Or call toll free: 888-549-8009**

DEVOTIONAL CDs

Chaplet of Divine Mercy
The traditional chant version sung by Vinny Flynn & daughters Colleen & Erin, featured for many years on EWTN. Over 80, 000 copies sold. **English CD $15.99 Spanish CD $14.99**

The Rosary & The Chaplet of Divine Mercy
Our best-selling CD. Includes recited versions of the Rosary and the Chaplet, with powerful meditations on the Passion from St. Faustina's diary. **$15.99**

Mother of Mercy Scriptural Rosary CD Set
"2010 Spoken Word Recording of the Year." This award-winning CD set by Vinny Flynn & Still Waters features a brief scripture reading before each Hail Mary to help you stay focused on the mysteries. Includes all 20 mysteries with beautiful background instrumental music. **2 CDs $17.99**

Mother of Mercy Scriptural Rosary Booklet
Pocket-sized booklet with beautiful, original illustrations for each of the 20 mysteries. Perfect for individual or group use, or as a companion to the 2-CD set. **$6.95**

The Gospel Rosary of Pope John Paul II
Our most compete rosary set, featuring long & short versions of each of the 20 mysteries. Dramatic readings from scripture, accompanied by beautiful background music, draw you into the Gospel events. **4 CDs $29.99**

The Complete Still Waters Rosary
A top seller. The short versions from each CD of the Gospel Rosary, remastered to fit on a single CD. Includes a brief meditation on each of the 20 mysteries. **$15.99**

Bring Vinny Flynn to Your Parish

Powerful Catholic Teachings , Music, and Prayer

Whether it's for a single talk at a conference or church event, a series of presentations for a retreat, or a full-blown parish mission, Vinny Flynn will help draw you to a fuller understanding of the truths of our faith and a deeper personal relationship with God.

Vinny Flynn:
Catholic teacher,
musician, and author
of *7 Secrets*
of the Eucharist

- Eucharistic Night of Healing
- Divine Mercy retreats
- Reconciliation evenings
- Parish Missions

For complete details, including parish program outline, talk descriptions, booking form, and promotional materials, go to: www.vinnyflynn.com or call toll free 877-737-2439.

"The Love That Saves"
© Maria Rangel, 2013, www.rangelstudios.com

 Maria Rangel pursued art as a career after graduating with a B.A. in Liberal Arts from Thomas Aquinas College in Santa Paula, CA. She also holds a B.F.A. in Fine Arts from the Laguna College of Art and Design in Laguna Beach, CA. She has grown in her insight and technique throughout her studies and has gained much inspiration from her time spent at the Angel Academy of Art in Florence, Italy. She now lives in Southern California with her husband and two sons.